5.⁰⁰

Ty[...]

Fill the Heavens with Commerce

Octave Chanute (U.S. AIR FORCE)

Fill the Heavens with Commerce

Chicago Aviation
1855-1926

by David Young and Neal Callahan

CHICAGO REVIEW PRESS

Library of Congress Cataloging in Publication Data

Young, David, 1940-
  Fill the heavens with commerce.

  Bibliography: p.
  Includes index.
  1. Aeronautics—Illinois—Chicago—History.
I. Callahan, Neal. II. Title.
TL522.I4Y68   629.13′09773′11   81-551
ISBN 0-914090-99-2   AACR2

First Edition
First Printing

ISBN cloth 0-914090-99-2
      paper 0-914091-00-x

Cover design and typography by
Siemens Communication Graphics

cover photo: This glider, designed by Russian-born Chanute assistant
William Paul Butusov, crashed upon launching from its trestle in late August,
1896. (NATIONAL AIR AND SPACE MUSEUM)

Published by Chicago Review Press, 820 N. Franklin, Chicago, IL 60610

Dedicated to four aviation pioneers of the era of the Aero Club of Illinois, Emil M. "Matty" Laird, Alfred O. Sporrer, C.R. "Sinnie" Sinclair and Don Lockwood.

Contents

List of Illustrations

Preface

The year after the Wright brothers' first successful flight in a heavier-than-air machine in 1903, a prominent Chicago civil engineer rose before the Western Society of Engineers and read a paper on aviation in which he predicted what effect the new machine would have on the scheme of things. The airplane would be successful, but would have a limited commercial application because of the relatively high cost of carrying goods by air. "They will not fill the heavens with commerce . . ." he predicted.

This man was Octave Chanute—builder of railroads, glider pioneer, chronicler of the infancy of aviation, and adviser to the Wrights. He could not have been more wrong about the possibilities of commercial flight, but this was a rare slip for Chanute. He was one of the handful of men who helped make airplanes a reality, and until his death in 1910 was probably the most prestigious member of the world's aviation community.

At the time of his death, Chanute was the head of a clique of wealthy men like Harold F. McCormick and Charles Dickinson who used their personal fortunes to establish Chicago as possibly the most important aviation center in the nation for a few years prior to World War I. The airport they established in Cicero was among the best equipped and purportedly the busiest flying field in the nation, and the lavish air shows they staged attracted the finest fliers.

The young men and women who learned to fly in Chicago or established it as their base of operations in those early years went on to become some of the best known figures in aviation—Glenn L. Martin, Chance Vought, Katherine Stinson, Allan Lougheed (later Lockheed), Shorty Schroeder, and Matty Laird.

The first in a long succession of Goodyear blimps was built in Chicago, and in 1919 one of those blimps crashed through the skylight of a Loop bank, causing what was probably the world's first civil aviation disaster. That disaster was the first in a succession of events that within a decade led to federal regulation of aviation.

By then, Chicago had become a center of the nation's air mail network—a position it would continue to hold for most of the Twentieth Century as commercial airlines supplanted the government Airmail Service. The city's geographical position which made it a center of marine and railroad activity also contributed to its development as an aviation hub. However, the existence of a well-financed aviation community in the city prior to 1920 undoubtedly contributed significantly to Chicago's emergence as an airline hub in the next decade. Several of the men who had their first brush with aviation at those primitive flying fields prior to 1920 went on to become organizers of both the federal Air Mail Service as well as promulgators of the new federal air safety regulations.

It would be misleading to state that Chicago was the early aviation center from which all innovation emanated; no such place existed. Once the Wrights had proven that powered flight was possible, aerialists the world over rushed back to their workshops and within the decade were producing all sorts of aircraft. However, what happened in the skies over Chicago between 1855 and 1926 is inseparable from the development of aviation elsewhere in the United States and in the world. Our book draws on heretofore unpublished records, including those of the Aero Club of Illinois, many photographs in private collections, and interviews with the scattering of aviation pioneers still alive to give what we feel is a rare portrait of aviation in its infancy and to document Chicago's role in the early development of flight.

Neal Callahan
David Young
Wheaton, Ill.
20 February, 1981

Acknowledgements

The authors thank Emil "Matty" Laird, C. R. "Sinnie" Sinclair, and Alfred O. Sporrer, three surviving aviation pioneers without whose guidance this book would not have been possible. Each donated material and photographs from their files, as well as many personal recollections of events.

Neil Mehler, one of the finest copyreaders in the business, proofread the manuscript and offered many suggestions to improve its clarity.

Also assisting by providing information and photographs were American, Delta, Eastern, Trans World and United airlines, especially Mary Rose Noel and James Casey of American and Jim McWayne of United. Other material was provided by Boeing Aircraft Company, Eaton Corporation, Goodyear Aerospace Corporation, Lockheed Corporation, Cliff Edwards of Heath Aircraft Company and Mike Berry, former manager of Midway Airport.

Individuals who helped gather information include Rufus Hunt, George Maxie, Roger Meyers, Mark Weaver, Cliff Condit, George Preister, Sid Pierson, George Niles, Chuck Downey, Owen B. Jones, Keehn Landis, Don Lockwood, Mrs. Quentin Krantz and Alfred Wolff.

The authors would also like to thank the historical societies of Chicago, repository of the Aero Club of Illinois records, Minnesota, Wisconsin, and Ohio for their assistance, as well as the Glenn Curtiss Museum, the Crawford Aviation Museum of the Western Reserve Historical Society and the Smithsonian Institution's National Air and Space Museum.

The Western Society of Engineers, Northwestern University libraries, the public libraries of Chicago and Evanston, Municipal Reference Library of Chicago, Forest Preserve District of Cook County, Chicago Park District, Federal Aviation Administration, Chicago Tribune, and the Aurora Beacon News also freely contributed material to the book.

A Note on the Title

The phrase "Fill the heavens with commerce" used by Octave
Chanute was probably borrowed from Alfred Lord Tennyson's
popular *Locksley Hall*:
> For I dipt into the future, far as human eye could see,
> Saw the Vision of the World, and all the wonder that would be;
>
> Saw the heavens fill with commerce, argosies of magic sails,
> Pilots of the purple twilight, dropping down with costly bales;
>
> Heard the heavens fill with shouting, and there rained a ghastly
> dew
> From the nations' air navies grappling in the central blue;

The poem was written between 1835 and 1842, and predicts not only
commercial aviation but aerial warfare. Curiously, at the time
Tennyson wrote Locksley Hall, fellow Englishmen William Samuel
Henson and John Stringfellow attempted to develop an airplane.
Henson in 1842 patented a flying machine called *Ariel*, and he and
Stringfellow formed the Aerial Transit Company to finance the
construction of a steam powered airplane. Both the plane and company
were ridiculed by the newspapers of the day, and neither got off the
ground.

The Aeronauts

Men had been flying in balloons for nearly a century when Washington Harrison Donaldson, a muscular, saturnine acrobat and trapeze artist, arrived in Chicago in the summer of 1875 in advance of P.T. Barnum's famous Roman Hippodrome. Donaldson's task was to whip up enthusiasm for the coming circus by drawing large crowds to a series of balloon ascensions. Although there had been several previous balloon flights in Chicago, one as early as 1855 and one by Donaldson in 1872, the novelty of flight was still sufficient to draw large crowds to watch Donaldson dangle from a trapeze suspended from a balloon.

Donaldson had many successful ascensions to his credit, despite a number of narrow escapes, but the 1875 flight in retrospect seemed doomed from the start. It was Donaldson's original intention to take several passengers on a flight across Lake Michigan—a feat never before attempted—but unfavorable winds on July 14 delayed the ascension. Donaldson actually got aloft with several passengers aboard, but was forced to return hastily to earth.

The next day, wind and rain from the southwest whipped up whitecaps on the lake, and it was discovered shortly before the scheduled takeoff that someone had inadvertently introduced air into the

1

balloon's hydrogen-filled bag, reducing its lift capacity. Donaldson decided to make the trip anyway, but with a lighter load. The original plan had been to take two newspaper reporters, James Maitland and Newton S. Grimwood, on the trip, but they were forced to draw for the lone available space. Anticipating that he would be gone for several days and would land somewhere in Michigan, Grimwood borrowed $10 from another reporter to pay for the return trip by train. There apparently was little reason for Grimwood to assume that anything would go wrong, despite the novelty of flight, because Donaldson had already survived 138 balloon ascensions all over the United States.

With Donaldson and Grimwood in the basket, the balloon rose slowly from Dearborn Park at Randolph Street and Michigan Avenue in the late afternoon and drifted on a breeze over Lake Michigan toward the northeast. A large crowd watched the balloon grow smaller and smaller until it disappeared in the distance. It was the last anyone would see of Donaldson.

Newspaper accounts of that time stated that just before dusk several persons aboard a lumber schooner 30 miles off Evanston noticed a balloon perilously close to the surface of the water. When they sailed to its assistance, the balloon unexpectedly gained altitude, as if it had suddenly been lightened of all ballast, and soared away to the northeast. Grimwood's body was discovered August 16 near Grand Haven, Michigan, his watch stopped at 11:20—presumably six hours and twenty minutes after the flight began—and his life jacket was badly torn. The few notes taken on the trip and found on his body gave no indication of what went wrong.[1]

Donaldson was presumed to have been lost in the lake, although his body and balloon were never recovered and persons who contended that they had seen him after the 1875 ascension kept popping up for years. One account published in the New York Times August 4, twenty-one days after the balloon's disappearance and twelve days before Grimwood's body was found, quoted a "reliable gentleman" as having seen Donaldson alive and well in Algonac, Michigan, a week after the balloon left Chicago. Another report quoted a man named Richard Dobson, of Marion, Indiana, who said he had seen Donaldson several years later making a balloon ascension in Scotland. Still

2

another account stated that years later some fishermen discovered on a remote island near Norway the badly deteriorated body of a man that had on one finger a ring bearing the inscription "Wash.D." Some lumberjacks in Michigan were also reported to have discovered a skeleton entangled in rope webbing similar to the type used to support the gondola of a balloon; however, they were lost at the time and were unable to lead authorities back to the site.

Whatever Donaldson's fate, his disappearance did not deter others from taking to the air in balloons, despite the risk. Probably the most serious drawback to balloons being used as airships was that because of their size they were vulnerable to the vagaries of weather, especially wind. Donaldson was involved in a series of accidents in his short, four-year career as an aeronaut that illustrate problems the early balloonists had with wind.

In 1872, he crashed into a smoke stack seventy-five feet above the ground in Columbus, Ohio, and later that year was unable to deflate properly his balloon upon landing in Chillicothe, Ohio, and was nearly dragged to his death in the wind. A few days later, during another ascension in Chillicothe, he struck a building, and the next month he tore a gas bag while attempting to land. He gained altitude too quickly on another flight, causing the hydrogen in the gas bag to expand too quickly and tear the netting supporting his trapeze. In yet another incident at Ironton, Ohio, he was swept away by high winds.

Wind, more than any other factor, has restricted balloons' contribution to the development of flight. Except for scientific experimentation and the evolution from balloon technology of such lighter-than-air ships as blimps and dirigibles, balloons remain today, as they were in Donaldson's time, primarily a novelty to be enjoyed by sportsmen wealthy enough to afford them.

The development of the gasoline engine and its application to balloons in the early Twentieth Century reduced their vulnerability to wind somewhat. Germany led the world in the development of powered lighter-than-air ships, like the gigantic zeppelins that bombed England during World War I and later circumnavigated the globe. However, by then it was too late. The development of the lightweight gasoline engine had already made possible the evolution of heavier-than-air machines that were faster, cheaper, and more flexible in their

Just exactly when this balloon ended up in the wires in this Chicago alley is unknown, but in 1912 such an incident did occur on the city's South Side. The balloon is the type built and flown from the White City Amusement Park in the early 1900's. (CHICAGO HISTORICAL SOCIETY)

uses than were dirigibles or blimps.

The development of balloons also was restricted by the gases used to inflate them and give them lift. Each gas used in balloons had its shortcomings. The first recognized balloon flights were made in 1783 by two Frenchmen under the patronage of ill-fated King Louis XVI, using heated air to give them lift. On June 5 of that year, brothers Jacques Etienne and Joseph Michel Montgolfier sent aloft a smoke-filled cloth bag, assuming it rose because smoke had lifting properties. They soon discovered that heated air, not smoke, gave balloons their lift.

The Montgolfiers then began sending animals aloft in hot air balloons, and on November 21, 1783, the king's historian, Francois Pilatre de Rozier, became the first man to fly when he ascended to an altitude of eighty-five feet for a minute and a half below a hot air balloon. The early French aeronauts quickly discovered the drawbacks of hot air balloons, however. The Montgolfiers used charcoal to heat the air, and there was always the danger than sparks would set the air bags afire. Hot air balloons also had a limited range because of the difficulty of keeping the air continuously hot.

Hydrogen was found to be a far more efficient gas in balloons, and within two months of de Rozier's first ascension, a man was sent aloft in a hydrogen-filled balloon. Despite the dangers of fire, hydrogen was the principal gas used in balloons and airships well into the Twentieth Century because it was readily available and had greater lift characteristics than other gases. Helium, an inert gas relatively immune to fire, was not isolated until the late Nineteenth Century and for several decades was too expensive to be used in balloons or airships. Besides, it did not have the lifting properties of hydrogen.

It was undoubtedly hydrogen that was used in Chicago's first recorded balloon flight, on July 4, 1855, when Silas M. Brooks took off from a vacant lot at Randolph and Peoria streets in *Eclipse* while a large crowd watched. Shortly after becoming airborne, however, Brooks realized that a west wind threatened to carry him out over the lake. He promptly released some gas from the balloon and descended onto the Michigan Southern Railroad (now Consolidated Rail Corporation) right-of-way, where the balloon became entangled in telegraph wires, sending Brooks and his gondola tumbling onto the tracks. The balloon, relieved of its ballast, suddenly shot skyward and drifted riderless out over Lake Michigan.[2]

The lake remained a threat to balloonists, and judging from the fact that aeronauts continued to be lost over the lake as late as the 1970s, it will probably remain a threat so long as men take to the air. Donaldson, one of the most famous balloonists of his time, narrowly escaped death in the lake in 1872 on his first ascension over Chicago. He drifted out over the lake and was rescued by an offshore craft.

John Wise was perhaps the nation's most respected aeronaut— the inventor of the ripping panel, a long seam near the top of the balloon that was torn open upon landing to enable the gas to escape and the balloon to stay on the ground. He was one of the organizers of the Union Army's balloon corps in the Civil War and in 1859 in the balloon *Jupiter*, the pilot of the first sanctioned air mail flight in the United States.[3] He fell victim to Lake Michigan four years after Donaldson. While attempting a long distance flight from St. Louis on September 29, 1879, his balloon crashed into the lake off Chicago's South Side and he and a passenger drowned.

The deaths of two of the nation's best known aeronauts did not deter ballooning in Chicago for long, however. Horace B. Wild performed often in 1903-10 from his balloon base in White City Amusement Park on Chicago's South Side, using a primitive dirigible propelled by a gasoline-powered Curtiss motorcycle engine. He apparently built his first airship in Chicago beginning in 1903 and ultimately completed fourteen. He went on to become a builder of heavier-than-air machines, but dropped from the aviation scene in the early 1920s after a series of scandals damaged his reputation.[4]

As late as 1908—five years after the invention of the airplane— balloons continued to draw large crowds in Chicago. On July 4 of that year, a crowd estimated at 150,000 persons in Jackson, Washington, and White City parks watched nine balloons ascend to begin the First International Aerial Race, an event held to break the world distance record for balloons of 872 miles then held by the German balloon *Pommera*. The largest balloon then in existence, the *Chicago*, which weighed 21,000 pounds and was owned by Charles O. Coey, president of the Aeronautique Club of Chicago, finished third in the race by flying 542 miles to Atwood, Ontario, in fourteen hours and forty

Horace B. Wild in his *Sky Buggy*, a powered airship, over Chicago in 1907. (CHICAGO HISTORICAL SOCIETY)

minutes. The *Fielding San Antonio*, owned by Dr. F.J. Fielding and flown by E. E. Honeywell, won the race by traveling 895 miles to West Sheffield, Quebec, in twenty-three hours and fifteen minutes.

That race was the culmination of sport ballooning in Chicago. By the time it was held, events had already occurred which would have profound effects on aviation in Chicago as well as the world. The most important was, of course, the development of the airplane by the Wright brothers, but before that happened a retired Chicago railroad construction engineer, Octave Chanute, conducted a series of glider experiments on the shore of Lake Michigan near what is today the site of Gary, Indiana. Chanute later provided the Wright brothers, by then involved in their own glider experiments, with the results of his tests and encouraged them in their effort to build an airplane.

1. *Chicago Tribune*, Nov. 5, 1899.
2. Brooks later recovered the air bag but found it was too deteriorated to attempt further flights. He went to Rockford, Ill., and built another balloon, the *Comet*, beneath which he performed in other Illinois cities for several years.
3. The flight took place between Lafayette and Crawfordsville, both in Indiana.
4. Wild's interesting career in aviation included building heavier-than-air machines with other members of the Aeronautique Club of Chicago, various activities sponsored by the Aero Club of Illinois, including the 1911 and 1912 air shows, and his own firm, the International Aircraft Co., 105 S. LaSalle St. He was arrested in 1917 for impersonating an Army captain, apparently while trying to sell stock in his company, and again in 1920 for receiving stolen government property. He died in 1940 in New York. *Chicago Tribune*, May 9, 1917; Aug. 11, 1920; Aug. 17, 1920; and March 15, 1924.

The Boys Have Done It

During much of the summer of 1896, the residents of the sleepy rural community of Miller Station, Indiana, on the southern shore of Lake Michigan, were alternately amused and puzzled by a series of strange goings-on atop nearby sand dunes. It was several years before United States Steel Corporation was to build its huge mills and name the place Gary, and Miller Station in those days was primarily used by vacationing Chicagoans and hunters of water fowl.

The normal routine was broken that summer by a group of four men who insisted upon dashing down the sides of sand dunes with strange-looking contraptions attached to their backs, leaping into the air, and gliding a few feet off the ground for several hundred feet. Occasionally the encampment was visited by newspaper reporters from nearby Chicago, who would be allowed to try their luck at gliding by the portly, white-bearded gentleman in charge.

That gentleman was Octave Chanute, and the gliding experiments he conducted at Miller Station[1] were instrumental in the development of powered flight. One of the glider designs tested by Chanute and his assistants that summer was to evolve within seven years as the airframe the Wright brothers flew in North Carolina to open the air age.

A Chanute glider kite during tests at Miller Beach, Ind., in 1896. (U.S. AIR FORCE)

Chanute had behind him a long and illustrious career in railroading when in 1889 he decided to retire, move to Chicago, and devote himself to his hobby—the mystery of flight. He was a methodical man, a civil engineer who had spent nearly forty years designing and building railroads and bridges across much of the United States, and unlike many of the aviation adventurers of that time who threw together contraptions to see whether they would fly, Chanute attacked the problem of building a heavier-than-air flying machine with his engineering skills. He first compiled the sum of mankind's knowledge of flight, analyzed it, and drew up a set of requisites that any flying machine must meet to be successful. He was then able to test his theories with unpowered gliders, and within a few years of launching his new career he had become one of the handful of men in the world[2] who set the stage for powered flight. Finally, he took the struggling Wright brothers under his wing when they were on the verge of abandoning their experiments, encouraged and advised them, and when they finally achieved success, spread the word of their discovery around the world.

Possibly his most important contribution was that for two decades he acted as the world's clearing house for aviation developments, publishing the results of others' work, as well as his own, so that experimenters the world over knew what was being done elsewhere, what had succeeded, and what had failed. His 1894 book, *Progress in Flying Machines*, may be the most important such work in the history of aviation[3].

Chanute's interest in flight apparently began in the 1850s when he began collecting as a hobby what information he could find on the subject. However, his interest went far beyond casually compiling facts, as an aviation buff might do today, to seriously studying the machines and the manner in which they were tested. After moving to Chicago in 1889, Chanute resumed his aviation studies on a full-time basis, and by May 2, 1890, was able to present to Sibley College of Engineering of Cornell University a lecture reviewing the developments of flight in balloons and heavier-than-air machines up to that time. He dismissed the theory that lighter-than-air machines would be developed for commercial transportation and opined that a successful heavier-than-air machine would consist of wings, or "aeroplanes," to sustain flight, and for propulsion have an "airscrew," or propeller, driven by a lightweight gasoline engine. He was convinced that such a machine would evolve from a succession of experiments conducted by different men, rather than from the efforts of a single genius working alone, and believed that a "working association of searchers" could best solve the riddle of flight.

By 1891, he published his comprehensive *Progress in Flying Machines* in a series of articles in *The American Railroad and Engineering Journal* and three years later reprinted it in book form. His descriptions in the book of unsuccessful and successful experiments as well as his discussions of why they failed or worked revealed to the aviation community for the first time the wasteful duplication that until then had characterized the tinkering of scores of experimenters each working alone with the trial-and-error method. Thus Chanute's book was a base from which future experimentation could progress without having to repeat the mistakes of the past.

Largely as a result of the serialized version of *Progress in Flying Machines*, an international conference on aerial navigation was organized in conjunction with Chicago's World's Columbian Exposition in 1893; Chanute was the keynote speaker to one hundred delegates from around the world. More important, the conference was the realization of Chanute's dream that a format was needed to permit the free exchange of ideas among the men who were trying to learn to fly.

After the conference, it occurred to Chanute that he would have to conduct experiments of his own to test the theories that he and the others had not resolved. He had been experimenting with model gliders and had been corresponding with Otto Lilienthal, a German who had been testing manned gliders and the first person to demonstrate that man could sail in the air by dangling from an airframe in a manner now common to hang gliders. However, Lilienthal used the method of shifting his body to maintain stability in flight, and Chanute was not satisfied that that was a practical method, especially when it came time to power the airframe. Chanute's inescapable conclusion was that he would have to build and test manned gliders to find a better system for maintaining stability. That led to the experiments at Miller Station in 1896 and 1897.

They began in December, 1895, when he and Augustus M. Herring, a young engineer interested in aviation who had recently worked with Samuel Pierpont Langley, secretary of the Smithsonian Institution in Washington and an early aviation experimenter, built glider models and a ladder kite. It was so named because it looked something like a step ladder with its many airfoils, or wings, piled one atop another to permit their reshuffling to test various theories. The kite proved stable in gusty winds, and the two men decided to build a glider capable of carrying a man. They actually built two machines; one was similar to the mono-wing Lilienthal glider and the other was a multiple-wing device based on the ladder kite.

In June 1896, Chanute, Herring, and assistants William A. Avery and William Paul Butusov established a camp at Miller Station to begin the tests. The first tested was the Lilienthal glider, which looked something like a giant bat. Herring and the others made 200 glides with it, one as long as 116 feet, before concluding that the 36-pound machine was too difficult to operate and control in the wind. Lilienthal died August 10, 1896—just a few weeks after the Chanute tests— after being injured the previous day in an experiment with one of his gliders at Rhinower Hills, near Stollen, Germany.

The other glider that Chanute had taken to Miller Station had twelve wings arranged in pairs above one another like the ladder kite. The original arrangement proved to be inefficient so the wing configuration was changed several times. Ultimately, about 200 glides were made, the longest being 82 feet. In early July, Chanute and his staff returned to Chicago to digest what had been learned. Despite the disappointing results, Chanute was convinced that "more had been learned during the two weeks of experiment with full-sized models than had previously been acquired during about seven years of theoretical study and experiments with models."[4]

Chanute and his assistants then built three more machines and returned to the Indiana dunes in late August to test them. The first to be tried was a new configuration of the multi-wing glider, which performed better than in the June-July tests but still proved to be inefficient. The second machine tested was a truss-wing biplane with a stabilizing tail designed by Herring. It was clearly the most successful machine tested; making glides of 150 to 360 feet,[5] the device proved

The most successful of Chanute's 1896 gliders, the truss-winged bi-plane, during trials on the dunes at Miller Beach, Ind. Note the similarity to the wing design of the Wright biplane. (U.S. AIR FORCE)

easy for the pilot to control simply by shifting his body and landed easily even when operated by some novices who appeared in camp.

The third glider tested, a bulky device designed by Butusov with 40-foot wings that had to be launched from a trestle, proved too cumbersome. It crashed into a tree on its second test flight.

The final tests on the dunes were conducted in September, 1897, when Chanute and Herring returned to further experiment with the biplane with the Herring tail.

With the experiments complete and conclusions in hand, Chanute proceeded to share what he had learned with the world, first in a paper read to the Western Society of Engineers and later in an article published in its journal. He held no illusions that his experiments alone would lead to flight, but continued to hold to the belief that it would be an evolutionary process to which many men would contribute and in which his role would be "advancing the question a little."[6]

His 1897 article and 1894 *Progress in Flying Machines* may have advanced the question even more than he realized. In May 1900, he received a letter from Wilbur Wright, who introduced himself by way of explaining that he and his brother, Orville, were experimenting with gliders and had read *Progress in Flying Machines*. Wright told Chanute he planned to experiment further with a kite glider using a system of wing warping for control and asked where the winds would be favorable for such tests. Chanute wrote back that San Diego, California, or Pine Island, Florida, would be preferable but that a number of locations along the Atlantic Coast would be acceptable.

His correspondence with the two young experimenters continued, and in June 1901, Chanute visited them in Dayton, Ohio. When he learned that they had conducted their glider experiments in 1900 near Kitty Hawk, North Carolina, without a doctor being present, he offered to pay the expenses of a physician to be on hand for the next round of tests. Chanute visited the Wright brothers at Kitty Hawk during another series of glider experiments later that year and talked a discouraged Wilbur Wright out of abandoning their work. He was impressed with the progress the Wrights had made and convinced Wilbur to go to Chicago on September 18, 1901, and discuss that progress before the Western Society of Engineers.

In 1903, Chanute spread the word of the Wrights' glider experiments to Europe on one of his frequent trips there. In a talk before the Aero Club of Paris, Chanute described his 1896-97 experiments, as well as those of the Wrights in 1901-02, and opined that the Wrights had practically solved the age old problem of equilibrium.[7]

After returning from Europe, he was invited to Kitty Hawk to watch the Wrights' first powered flight. He arrived November 6, 1903, but the cold weather and his age (he was 71) forced him to leave in less than a week. He was at his Chicago home at 1138 N. Dearborn St., on Thursday, December 17, when he received the historic news by telegram from Katharine Wright, Orville and Wilbur's sister:

"The boys have done it."

They had not done it without some help, however. As Chanute had predicted, the development of the airplane was an evolutionary process. Major refinements in the basic design and structure of aircraft continued for many years after the Wrights first flew their airplane.

The evolution of the airplane perhaps is best illustrated by the development of the stabilizing devices necessary to control the aircraft in flight. Whereas the development of the truss wing design used in early biplanes, including the Wright machines, was relatively simple in view of Chanute's background in railroad bridge construction, the age old problem of aeronautical stability, or equilibrium, as Chanute called it, was not, and based on the rather poor results of the experimenters to that date, the problem was incompletely understood.

Chanute as early as May 2, 1890, in a lecture at Cornell University theorized that the problem of equilibrium in flight would have to be tested on "self starting," or drone, aircraft before men could take to the air in machines. By 1896, when Chanute was involved in his experiments, he became convinced that a self-stabilizing machine was possible, rejecting the hang gliding theories of Lilienthal. The stabilizing tail structure apparently designed by one of his assistants, Augustus Herring,[8] and added to the Chanute biwing glider was an attempt to create such a self-stabilizing machine. The device provided some stability under optimum conditions, but still required the glider pilot to shift his body to steer the craft in unfavorable winds— an impossibility in powered flight.

The next step was taken by the Wrights, who developed a system of wing warping whereby a system of cables controlled by the pilot distorted the wing tips to stabilize and steer the aircraft. However, such a system was cumbersome and virtually impossible to maintain on a monoplane.

The next major step in the evolutionary process was accomplished by the group working with Glenn Curtiss[9] in 1908 when they installed on the wings of their airplanes the trailing edge control surfaces known as ailerons, which were also operated by the pilot. Ailerons were patented in the United Kingdom by Michael Boulton as early as 1868—long before there was any need for them—but were not practically utilized on aircraft before 1908.

Chanute continued to publish prolifically on the subject of flight even after the 1903 success of the Wrights, and he was probably more responsible than anyone else for spreading the word around the globe that someone had finally solved the problem of powered flight, and how. He always seemed to place the latest accomplishment in its proper perspective, although in 1904 he made a statement in a paper read before the Western Society of Engineers that has amused and disturbed aviation historians ever since because in it he seemed to have forsaken powered flight just after its birth:

> Flying machines promise better results as to speed, but yet will be of limited commercial application. They may carry mail and reach inaccessible places, but they can't compete with railroads as carriers of passengers or freight. They will not fill the heavens with commerce, abolish customs houses, or revolutionize the world, for they will be too expensive for the loads which they carry, and subject to too many wind contingencies. Success, however, is probable.[10]

The comment was interpreted as a concession by the old man to the railroad industry that he served so well for decades, but upon closer examination indicates that Chanute was simply trying to place the airplane into the role it would fill for the remainder of the Twentieth Century. He was clearly wrong in his prediction that the airplane could not compete with the passenger train as a carrier of people; however, that role was taken by the automobile. Nonetheless, the railroads remained the primary carriers of freight in the nation, and for the reason stated by Chanute: airplanes are too expensive for the loads they carry. In fact, the greatest competitor of the railroads for freight during the bulk of the Twentieth Century was not the airplane but the truck.

Although Chanute is probably best known for his contributions to aviation, his work in railroading was sufficient to give him a prominent place in the history of that industry. He was born February 18, 1832, in Paris, the son of a professor of history at the Royal College of France, and was brought to the United States six years later when his father became vice president of Jefferson College in Louisiana. The family moved to New York City in 1844, and by 1849, Chanute, then 17 years old and, to use his words, "thoroughly Americanized," applied for a job on the Hudson River Railroad, then under construction. When told that there were no jobs available, he volunteered to the railroad's resident engineer at Sing Sing, New York, to work without pay. Within two months he was on the payroll at $1.12 a day.

Chanute headed west in 1853 after construction of that railroad was completed and landed a job surveying and building the railroad line between Joliet, Illinois, and Bloomington, Illinois (now the Illinois Central Gulf), then became engineer in charge of building what is today the Toledo, Peoria & Western Railroad between Peoria, Illinois, and the Indiana State Line.

When that was completed, he went on to a succession of railroad jobs in the Midwest between 1861 and his return to New York City in 1873. In 1867, he submitted the winning design in a contest to plan the Chicago Union Stockyards; in 1867, he built the first railroad bridge over the Missouri River; and in 1871, he designed the Kansas City Stockyards. After his return to the East to rebuild the Erie Railroad, Chanute served in his spare time in 1873-75 on a five-member committee of the American Society of Civil Engineers to plan New York City's first rapid transit elevated system. The committee, on which Chanute was the driving force, not only proposed that four lines be built but, contrary to the opinion of the city's financial community, produced an economic analysis showing that they could be profitably operated. Chanute, who worked on the 4,000-page report at night because his railroad duties kept him busy during the day, was so exhausted upon its completion that he took a vacation to Europe.

However, the report so impressed his colleagues in the American Society of Civil Engineers that in 1880 he was appointed chairman of a committee to study ways to improve the preservation of wood used in great quantities by railroads for crossties, bridges, and telegraph poles. Five years later he reported that the best preservation possible was by impregnation with creosote oil—a method still in use today. He moved to Kansas City in 1883 to head his own consulting firm and design steel railroad bridges for the Atchison, Topeka & Santa Fe Railway over both the Missouri and Mississippi Rivers.

After his retirement from railroading in 1889, Chanute's primary interest was aviation, and he remained an avid booster of flying until his death. He was present on October 16, 1909, with Harold F. McCormick and Charles Dickinson—two men who would be important in the subsequent development of aviation in Chicago—when pioneer aviator Glenn Curtiss flew his 400-pound biplane for one-fourth mile over the infield at Hawthorne Race Track in west suburban Cicero. It was the first recorded airplane flight in the Chicago area, and it rekindled the city's dormant interest in aviation, which until that day had focused primarily on Chanute's writings. The flight was scheduled for October 15, but high winds prevented Curtiss from taking off. He was talked into addressing the Chicago Automobile Club instead of flying, and with Chanute, McCormick, and Dickinson in attendance he urged the formation of an aero club in Illinois to promote the development of aviation.

It took Chanute, McCormick, and Dickinson just four months from the time of Curtiss' suggestion to form the Aero Club of Illinois. Chanute was elected its first president in February, 1910.

His tenure was short. Chanute, then 78, became ill while traveling in Europe that summer and returned to Chicago. He never regained his health, and died November 23, 1910.[11]

1. The site is now marked by a plaque adjacent to the field house in Gary's Marquette Park.

2. Other important pre-Wright experimenters included Samuel Pierpont Langley of the Smithsonian Institution, Germany's Otto Lilienthal, and Louis Pierre Mouillard in Cairo, Egypt.

3. Wilbur Wright, writing in tribute after Chanute's death in 1910, said:

If he had not lived, the entire history of progress in flying would have been other than it has been, for he encouraged not only the Wright brothers to persevere in their experiments, but it was due to his missionary trip to France in 1903 that the Voisins, Bleriot, DeLaGrange, and Archdeacon were led to undertake a revival of aviation studies in that country, after the failure of the efforts of Adler and the French government in 1897 had left everyone in idle despair. Although his experiments in automatic stability did not yield the results which the world has yet been able to utilize, his efforts had vast influence in bringing about the era of human flight. His 'double-deck' modifications of the old Wenham and Stringfellow machines will influence flying machine design as long as flying machines are made.

4. Chanute, *Glider Experiments*, Oct. 20, 1897, address to the Western Society of Engineers as published in the Society's Journal.

5. The Wright brothers' first powered flight on Dec. 17, 1903, was 120 feet long.

6. Chanute in his Oct. 20, 1897, address listed ten principal problems that must be resolved before powered flight was possible:

a. Supporting power and resistance to air.

b. The motor.

c. The propeller.

d. Form and kind of apparatus—the airframe.

e. Extent of sustaining surfaces—the wings.

f. Material and texture of apparatus.

g. Maintenance of equilibrium.

h. Guidance in any desired direction.

i. Starting up under all conditions.

j. Alighting safely anywhere.

7. With the Wright developments in retrospect, Chanute published in the June, 1907, *American Magazine of Aeronautics* another list of flight prerequisites:

a. Equilibrium.

b. Ability to steer—both horizontally and vertically.

c. Adequate amount and shape of sustaining surface, or the weight of the aircraft per square foot of wing surface. A high weight to area ratio requires greater speed to sustain flight.

d. Least possible resistance to framing of hull, with the head, or front, resistance equal to the drift, or side, resistance.

e. Lightest possible motor in relation to its power.

f. Most efficient propeller.

g. Learning to fly. (He recommended that pilots learn to glide before attempting powered flight.)

8. Augustus M. Herring was one of the most enigmatic figures in American aviation history, a man constantly working with but in the shadow of Langley, Chanute, and Curtiss. Some of his proponents claim Herring

successfully flew a powered machine on Oct. 11, 1898, on a beach near St. Joseph, Mich., after the 1896-97 glider experiments with Chanute. However, Herring himself apparently made no serious claim to having upstaged the Wright brothers. Herring invited Chanute to St. Joseph on Oct. 16 to witness a second experiment, but the machine was somehow damaged before Herring could get it into the air, and Chanute returned to Chicago with serious doubts about his former colleague. Herring claimed to have successfully negotiated several short hops with the machine after Chanute's departure. He died July 17, 1926.

Although a number of other inventors have been advanced by their proponents as having flown powered machines before the Wrights, the development of the airplane can be directly traced to the Wrights because of their patent of the method used by pilots to control aircraft in flight. Unlike Chanute and Herring, who dabbled with a self-stabilizing system, the Wrights developed a system of cables to enable the pilot to warp the wings in flight to attain control.

9. Glenn Hammond Curtiss, a motorcycle enthusiast and builder of lightweight engines for those vehicles, was actually induced into aviation by Alexander Graham Bell, inventor of the telephone and early enthusiast of flying. In 1907, Bell formed the Aerial Experiment Association and enlisted Curtiss as director of experiments; Army Lieutenant Thomas E. Selfridge (later killed in a crash of a Wright plane), as secretary; Frederick W. Baldwin, as chief engineer; and John A.D. McCurdy, as his assistant.

Encouraged by Bell, the group built and tested several flying machines at Hammondsport, N.Y. The group eventually disbanded, and Curtiss, in company with Augustus M. Herring, formed the first aircraft manufacturing firm in the United States. He became the Wrights' chief rival in American aviation, developing seaplanes, training pilots, and, as early as 1910, introducing the idea of the aircraft carrier.

10. *Popular Science Monthly*, March, 1904.

11. He was buried in Peoria.

Chicago's first operable airplane was bought in 1909 from Glenn Curtiss by automobile dealer James Plew. Otto Brodie, the city's first pilot, and Horace B. Wild are shown pushing it. (C.R. SINCLAIR COLLECTION)

The Flying Machine Comes to Chicago

Chicago was just awakening to the era of powered flight when the Aero Club of Illinois was organized on February 10, 1910. In the six years that had elapsed since the Wrights first flew their airplane, the motley handful of tinkerers in Chicago who tried to emulate their accomplishment met with very limited success. Only one of the twelve inventors who obtained patents on aeronautical devices between 1900 and 1910 is believed to have produced a practical airplane; he was Carl S. Bates, a Chanute disciple.[1] More typical of the aeronautical inventors of the day was James F. Scott, a scenic artist by trade, who was low bidder on a government contract to develop an airplane but defaulted when he discovered his bid price could not cover his costs. Chicago's first recorded airplane flight did not occur until almost six years after the Wrights's flight, when Glenn Curtiss came from St. Louis to demonstrate his airplane and urge the formation of an aero club.

However, the Aero Club, which was run by a small group of men with wealth and prestige at their disposal, profoundly influenced aviation in Chicago for two decades. Within two years they had established Chicago as a world aviation center, possessor of what was at the time the country's best airport, and source of such aviation pioneers as Chance Vought, Glenn Martin, Victor Lougheed (later Lockheed), Katherine Stinson, William B. Stout, and Emil (Matty) Laird.

But in the winter of 1910 the organizers of the club hardly seemed to know what to do with their new organization. The venerable but feeble Chanute was elected the club's first president, to be succeeded nine months later after his death by James E. Plew, the Chicago agent for the White Steam Car Company and Curtiss-manufactured airplanes.

The club's other officers included Harold F. McCormick, heir to the McCormick reaper fortune; Robert M. Cutting; Charles E. Barrett; and Victor Lougheed, a member of the family that, after changing its name to Lockheed, founded the aircraft company.

While the club struggled to find itself, the principal promoters of aviation of that day remained the newspapers. William Randolph Hearst made an offer of $50,000 to the first man to fly coast to coast, and the *New York World* and *St. Louis Post-Dispatch* posted a reward of $30,000 to anyone who could fly between those cities. Glenn Curtiss collected $10,000 from the *World* for flying between Albany and New York City, a distance of 141 miles, in two hours and fifty-one minutes. Four days later, J.C. Shaffer, publisher of the *Chicago Evening Post*, offered $1,000 to the first person to fly between Chicago and New York. The *Chicago Record Herald* topped that with an offer of $10,000 for a flight between Chicago and Springfield, Illinois, and the *Post* then raised its offer to $25,000.

Meanwhile, Aero Club members McCormick and Charles Dickinson, the wealthy vice president of a seed company, went to New York City the last week of October, 1910, to watch an air show held at Belmont Park. Dickinson took his first airplane ride at the show, reportedly paying pilot Claude Graham-White, winner of the 1910 Gordon Bennett Race, $500 for the flight. Most important, McCormick and Dickinson came away with the conviction that a spectacular air show was probably the fastest way to generate interest in aviation in Chicago.

At the Aero Club board meeting March 6, 1911, in the Chicago Athletic Association, McCormick's suggestion prevailed that a major aviation meet should be held in Chicago that year. The directors agreed that the club should sponsor the event, then adjourned to Grant Park to determine whether it would be suitable as the site. Apparently there were no serious objections, because it was chosen.

The principal problem then became raising enough money to finance the prizes that would be necessary to attract well-known aviators from throughout the world. McCormick and James E. Plew invited almost every prominent businessman in Chicago to a fund-raising dinner April 6 in the Blackstone Hotel to hear famed balloonist Augustus Post, a founder of the Aero Club of America, speak and show lantern slides of the 1910 Belmont show.

In the end, however, McCormick became the show's principal financial backer, advancing the club $45,000 in cash and putting up his personal bond for $80,000 in prize money and the bonding of several foreign machines for the show.[2]

McCormick was as unlikely an aviation pioneer as Chicago has had. He was a member of one of the city's patrician families, dominated its social life, and spent as much time as possible in Europe. Yet from 1910 through 1915 there probably was no more important person in aviation in Chicago, primarily because he committed much of his family's wealth to getting the aviation community on a sound footing.

He was born Mary 2, 1872, the son of Cyrus Hall McCormick, inventor of the mechanical reaper, founder of International Harvester Company, and one of the Chicago industrialists who made his fortune by harnessing the wealth of the vast prairie that stretched for a thousand miles westward. Young Harold McCormick received all the benefits of his father's wealth. He attended Princeton University, where he played football; soon after his graduation in 1895 he married Edith Rockefeller, daughter of oil monopolist John D. Rockefeller. For many years, the McCormicks ruled Chicago society, lavishing money on their favorite causes, such as the opera, to which they gave an estimated five million dollars.

McCormick's interest in aviation can be traced to 1901, when he was visiting Paris shortly after the death of his eldest son, John Rockefeller McCormick, and watched the famed Brazilian dare-devil Alberto Santos-Dumont fly his powered racing balloon around the Eiffel Tower to collect a 100,000-franc prize. The spectacle obviously interested McCormick, for he later wrote to an intermediary in Paris asking him to obtain from Dumont a photograph or drawing of the balloon. Santos-Dumont refused.

His interest was rekindled in Chicago eight years later when he watched with Chanute and Dickinson as Curtiss made the Chicago area's first airplane flight and urged formation of an aero club. Thus the seed was sown, and McCormick committed his prestige and much of his fortune to the development of aviation. It is uncertain whether he viewed it solely as a diversion or considered it a potentially lucrative industry in which he could make another fortune. In addition to backing the 1911 air show, McCormick attempted to start an airline, designed an unsuccessful airplane, and donated to the Aero Club some land in the western suburbs for use as an airport.

After 1912, McCormick's interest turned from land-based planes to seaplanes, or hydroplanes, as they were called in those days. He bought his own flying boat from Curtiss and used it occasionally to commute from his home in Lake Forest, where he erected hangars on his private beach, twenty-eight miles to his office in downtown Chicago. He also unsuccessfully attempted in 1914 to start a commuter airline carrying passengers in hydroplanes between Lake Forest, other north shore suburbs, and Chicago.

After 1914, his interest in aviation waned. He and his wife spent most of their time in Europe from 1915 through late 1918, when he assumed the presidency of International Harvester Company upon the retirement of his brother, Cyrus. Apparently his executive duties left little time for aviation, for he never attempted to revive his previous interests.

From then on, various romantic associations ruined his first marriage and involved him in a great deal of public notoriety. Press reports of the day said he was duped out of considerable money by a young woman who claimed she was the daughter of the Sultan of Turkey. In 1921 he was divorced by his first wife, and the next year he married Ganna Walska, a Polish opera singer. They were divorced in 1931, and seven years later he married a California woman and spent most of the rest of his life in that state. He died October 16, 1941.

But in 1911, most of McCormick's energies were devoted to over-coming obstacles to the Aero Club's proposed air show. In addition to the problem of raising money, the Wright brothers proved to be un-willing participants. The development of aviation in the United States from 1903 to 1908 was retarded by the inability of the Wrights to obtain a patent on their flying machine and their understandable reluctance to share information about it until it could be protected.[3] Once the patent, number 821,393, was granted, the courts gave it broad interpretation, holding that it covered not only flying machines using the Wright-developed wing warping method of control but also those using ailerons.

Before the Chicago air show, the Wrights had secured from Judge John R. Hazel of Federal District Court in Buffalo, New York, a tem-porary restraining order (January 3, 1910) against Curtiss and the Herring-Curtiss Company, although the matter was held in abeyance while on appeal. The Wrights had charged in their complaint that Curtiss' *June Bug* aircraft, although equipped with ailerons, was an infringement on their patent.[4] In effect, the Wrights were attempting to restrict the manufacture of airplanes in the United States and Europe except under license to them.

The possibility that the Aero Club of Illinois would be forced to pay the Wrights a license fee to hold an aviation meet so concerned its members that on April 14, 1911, the club sent a delegation consisting of John T. McCutcheon, *Chicago Tribune* cartoonist and early avia-tion promoter, and McCormick to Dayton to discuss the financial aspects of such a license. The Wrights provided McCutcheon with his first airplane ride, but demanded $10,000 to license the meet as well as financial guarantees to each Wright pilot who appeared.

"He (Orville Wright) very openly stated there were three things he wanted: First, to prevent foreign aviators from coming to America. Second, to get as much money out of the meet as possible. Third, to support his patents. He stated that our meet was a detriment to them rather than a gain. He stated that he did not care whether aviation in America was helped or not," wrote McCormick in his report to the Aero Club on the meeting in Dayton. "He (Orville Wright) stated he would now sue every aviator they could afford to and their only reason for not doing so was because it cost them too much money,"

McCormick continued.[5]

Anticipating the possibility of a lawsuit, the Aero Club the same month formed the International Aviation Meet Association, a non-profit organization put together in the event the Wrights attempted court action to block the meet or sought damages. Plew was appointed president of IAMA, McCormick was on its executive committee, and Dickinson was a general committee member. McCormick proposed that IAMA protect itself from the possibility that the Wrights would attempt to drive away other aviators and claim all the $80,000 in prizes for themselves by requiring that before any prizes be awarded, a certain number of aviators representing different interests be entered in the meet.

The Wrights promptly sent a letter to Bernard Mullaney, general manager of IAMA, warning that any patent infringements would be dealt with in court. "As the parties exhibiting machines and holding meets where infringing machines are exhibited become themselves infringers. . . . " wrote F.H. Russell, manager of the Wright Company.[6]

However, sentiment was building in Chicago to ignore the Wrights' demands. Mullaney described the Wrights' position as a "dog in the manger policy which should not be encouraged" and urged other air meet organizers in the United States to band together and draft a cooperative defense against the Wrights.[7] By that time the dispute between IAMA and the Wrights had attracted national attention, and the Wrights were publicly criticized by aviation organizations in several states. Finally on July 28, the Aero Club of America gave its official sanction to the meet, but inquiries from concerned aviators and companies continued to arrive in Chicago almost to the eve of the August 12-20, 1911, meet. The Burgess Company and Curtiss, of Marblehead, Massachusetts, wrote Mullaney that if the meet were not licensed by the Wrights, they would be forced to pay $100 a day for each airplane entered and urged IAMA to agree to cover those expenses.[8]

McCormick and other officials of the Aero Club decided that they would resist the Wrights' demands, although they were aware that such refusal to pay the licensing fees was a gamble. They desperately needed the Wright planes and pilots to make the meet a success and correctly guessed that the meet would be so financially attractive that the Wrights could not boycott it even if they did go to court to stop it. The Aero Club's officials also correctly surmised that the Wrights would have a better chance in court if they sued the pilots and aircraft companies instead of the non-profit IAMA. Most of the aviators ultimately paid the $100 a day licensing fee to take a chance on winning part of IAMA's large purse.[9]

The other major problem facing the meet's organizers was the habit of aviators to demand substantial guarantees to fly in such events. The presence of the most famous men in aviation was necessary to insure the meet's success, and these men usually demanded the largest guarantees. As early as April 17, slightly more than a month after the decision was made to hold the meet, the famed English flier T.O.M. Sopwith asked for a $5,000 guarantee in advance. Earl Ovington, of Massachusetts, asked for $6,000 in guarantees to fly. Others who expressed interest in the meet included Canada's J.A.D. McCurdy, Charles Willard, France's Rene Barrier, Russia's Abraham Raygordsky, and native Chicagoan St. Croix Johnstone.

The Aero Club decided there would be no guarantees other than a $250 stipend per aviator to cover expenses. The club's officials correctly assumed that the $80,000 purse would lure the world's best fliers, and even the Wrights sent a team to compete.

Even while the financial and legal problems were being negotiated, Aero Club members proceeded with the planning of the technical details of the meet, a process that took months. Seats were built for 63,000 spectators, and the runway and 1.33-mile race course was designed and prepared by James S. Stephens, an Aero Club member. The club had to procure a large amount of castor oil to lubricate the Gnome engines used on airplanes in the meet, as well as mark a mock battleship hull on the ground in Grant Park for the aviators to bomb with bags filled with flour. Hangars were built in the park, and Pinkerton agents were hired to guard the planes.

The association also procured a small platform scale with which passengers could be weighed because most of the pilots entered planned to make money on the side by giving airplane rides to the public. The federal government ordered the Coast Guard cutter *Tuscarora*, normally stationed in Milwaukee, temporarily assigned to Chicago for the meet, and a detachment of troops from Fort Sheridan to

29

be on hand to control the crowds. An artillery detachment from Fort Riley, Kansas, was ordered to Chicago to provide signal guns, and a Signal Corps unit was detailed to provide wireless service.

Then for nine days in August, 1911, the world aviation community turned its attention to Chicago.

1. Howard L. Scamehorn, *Balloons to Jets*, Henry Regnery Co., Chicago, 1951, p. 44.

2. Grover Sexton, Aero Club secretary, letter of Aug. 18, 1911 in Aero Club files in the possession of the Chicago Historical Society.

3. Rodney K. Worrel, *The Wright Brothers' Pioneer Patent, American Bar Association Journal*, October, 1979, pp. 1512-18.

4. The U.S. Court of Appeals finally upheld the Wrights' patent on Jan. 13, 1914.

5. Harold F. McCormick, report submitted to Aero Club on June 23, 1911, in Aero Club files.

6. F.H. Russell, letter of July 5, 1911, in Aero Club files.

7. Bernard Mullaney, letter of July 6, 1911, in Aero Club files.

8. Burgess Company and Curtiss letter of July 17, 1911, in Aero Club files.

9. The Wright Company finally filed a suit against the International Aviation Meet Association on Aug. 17, 1911—five days after the meet began—alleging patent infringements. The civil complaint was never pursued by the Wrights, although the IAMA after the meet set aside $10,000 in a special escrow account to cover any damages that might be adjudged against the association.

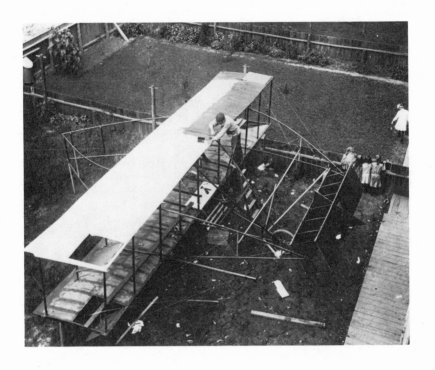

Typical of the earliest aviators was J. E. Mair, who built this biplane in the back yard of his home at 3106 W. Fullerton Ave., Chicago, in 1910. There is no record that it ever flew. (CHICAGO HISTORICAL SOCIETY)

31

The 1911 Air Show

Several hundred thousand persons were on hand in the Grant Park area on August 12, 1911, to watch what had thus far been the largest extravaganza in the brief history of aviation—the Chicago International Aviation Meet. The city's newspapers had promoted the event heavily and the non-profit corporation sponsoring the meet had spent more than $19,000 on advertising and publicity. The *Chicago Tribune* carried a supplement August 8 explaining what was about to take place, the status of aviation to that day, and even a speculative article on possibilities of space travel.[1]

Many businesses in the city conducted promotions. Hotels along Michigan Avenue overlooking the park advertised the view from their rooms and quickly sold out for the week; Marshall Field & Company, the department store, printed daily programs and displayed two airplanes the week of the meet. The location of the meet undoubtedly contributed to its success: Grant Park was adjacent to Chicago's central business district and easily accessible to the city's elevated transit system, commuter railroads, and intercity passenger trains. Never before or since has an aviation meet of that magnitude been held in the downtown area of one of the world's major cities.

33

Grandstand and general admission tickets on sale in the Auditorium Theater, downtown stores, and hotels were sold for fifty cents to two dollars, depending upon the location of the seats, and automobile parking cost one dollar. The show began at 3:30 p.m. each day, and many businesses let their employees out early to watch. The day's events started with a flight duration contest, followed by a race over a three-and-a-half-mile course over the lake at 4:30 p.m., biplane passenger carrying races at 5:30 p.m., altitude competition at 6 p.m., and cross-country flying at 7 p.m. Before the beginning of events each day, many of the pilots earned pocket money by giving Chicagoans plane rides, some reportedly charging several hundred dollars for a few minutes in the air.

Opening day, August 12, a Saturday, provided its share of thrills for the crowd. Because of frequent malfunctions on the primitive and fragile aircraft, pileups were common, although the relatively slow flying speed of airplanes of that day meant that few crashes were fatal. On the first day, Arthur Stone crashed in his Queen Bleriot monoplane when, on making a steep turn at low altitude, a wing hit the ground, flipping the plane on its back. He was unhurt. Frank Coffyn and two passengers in his Wright biplane escaped injury when he made a forced landing and struck another plane sitting on the field. Rene Simon's Moisant went out of control, hitting a tree, after the engine was started.[2] James Martin overshot a landing in his Bristol-Farman biplane and hit a fence. Neither he nor Simon was injured.

The winners the first day included Earle Ovington, who defeated Britain's T.O.M. Sopwith in the speed races by flying twenty miles in twenty-three minutes and fifty-two seconds. Howard Gill won the altitude contest, attaining 4,980 feet in his Wright biplane to defeat Lincoln Beachey (3,507 feet), and Phillip Parmelee (3,273 feet). Calbraith P. Rodgers was first in the duration contest by staying airborne for two hours, fifty-five minutes, and thirty-three seconds.[3]

The next day, Sunday, an estimated four hundred thousand persons crowded into downtown Chicago to watch the meet. Part of the crowd could get no closer to Grant Park than State Street, two blocks to the west in the middle of the city's mercantile district, and traffic on nearby streets was halted when wagon drivers and motorists temporarily abandoned their vehicles to get a closer look. Spectators

The pit area of the International Aviation Meet in 1911 in Grant Park. The monoplane at the right was the one flown by French pilot Rene Simon. The Chicago Yacht Club building is in the background. (CHICAGO HISTORICAL SOCIETY)

crowded onto bridges over the Illinois Central Railroad right-of-way on the western edge of the park, lined the tops of buildings along Michigan Avenue, hung out hotel windows, climbed lamp posts, and perched atop signs to get a better view.

Those close enough to see what was happening were not disappointed. An unexpected gust of wind caused J.J. Frisbie's plane to brush a statue atop the 250-foot Montgomery Ward Building, and Frisbie, who injured his hand in the collision, temporarily lost control of the plane. It spiraled downward for a few seconds before he was able to regain control with his uninjured hand and land safely. Beachey skimmed over the tops of cars on Michigan Avenue, made turns at such low altitudes that his wheels touched the ground, and continued with his other crowd-thrilling aerobatics.

The highlight of the activities on August 14, Monday, was the arrival of Boston aviator Harry Atwood on the third leg of his cross-country flight from St. Louis to New York City in an effort to claim a $10,000 prize. Atwood left St. Louis at 8:40 a.m., and with stops in Springfield and Pontiac for fuel, made the 260-mile flight to Chicago in six hours and twelve minutes. He left Grant Park the next day and landed in New York August 25 without having to make any major repairs on his machine on the 1,266-mile trip—something of a record in itself considering the primitive state of aircraft engines in that age.

The aviators in the meet continued their charmed existence August 14, despite five accidents. Rene Simon was skimming over the lake in his Moisant when the engine failed and he glided to a crash landing in the water. Hugh A. Robinson at the time was airborne in his Curtiss hydro-aeroplane, the only flying boat at the meet, and landed on the lake near the downed flier. Robinson taxied across the water to a place at which Simon could hold onto the flying boat, but he refused to leave the scene until a tug boat attached lines to his downed plane and pulled it ashore. The incident may have been the first practical air-sea rescue in history.

A more serious accident occurred later in the day when Lee Hammond's Baldwin biplane lost a wire as he rounded a water intake crib three and a half miles out in the lake. The loose wire fouled his propeller, but Hammond was able to jump free of the airplane just before it crashed into the water. He was rescued by a boat posted nearby.

36

Ovington also piled up his Curtiss plane when the engine failed while he was rounding a pylon in the park, but he was unhurt and within fifteen minutes was airborne again in a spare Bleriot.

The incredible luck of the aviators ran out the next day, August 15, when the meet suffered its only two fatalities. William R. Badger, 27, of Pittsburgh, died when his plane crashed in a dive. Trying to surpass a stunt by Beachey, Badger attempted a 300-foot dive but tried to pull out of it only twenty feet off the ground. He was crushed in the wreckage. The accident was witnessed from the air by John T. McCutcheon, the *Tribune* cartoonist, who had been offered an airplane ride by Orville Wright and was flying above the field with pilot Frank T. Coffyn when Badger went down.

McCutcheon was airborne again with Coffyn two hours later when Chicagoan St. Croix Johnstone, 26, crashed in his monoplane in the lake and drowned. McCutcheon recalled later that he watched transfixed as an ambulance sped across Grant Park toward the lake, where Johnstone's plane could still be seen just below the surface. Another pilot said the plane seemed to have exploded at 1,600 feet before diving straight into the water. Robinson, who was again aloft in his flying boat at the time, attempted another air-sea rescue by landing near where Johnstone's plane had disappeared into forty feet of water. Robinson waited anxiously for Johnstone to free himself and bob to the surface; however, he must have been trapped in the wreckage or too seriously injured by the explosion. Robinson stood by until divers freed the body. The surviving aviators flew an extra day (August 21) after the official end of the meet to raise money for Johnstone's widow.

The two deaths brought an immediate outcry that the remainder of the meet be cancelled, especially by Dr. Stuart Johnstone, father of the dead aviator. Dr. Johnstone issued a public appeal to stop the "carnage," but IAMA officials decided to proceed with the rest of the meet, contending that many aviators had come long distances to participate and the meet was important in increasing knowledge of aviation. The remainder of the meet was completed without another fatality, although mishaps continued to occur.

Probably the biggest single problem to aviators was the wind. The airplane of that day was little more than a light-weight glider powered by a gasoline engine and capable of average speeds of slightly more than fifty miles an hour. The Wright Company forbade its pilots to fly in strong winds, although Beachey and Eugene Ely,[4] both flying Curtiss aircraft, got their planes into the air on at least one day when no one else would attempt flying. A strong wind from the west proved to be the most troublesome for pilots because of the geography of Grant Park, bounded on the west by tall buildings, which made a takeoff into the wind impossible, and on the east by the lake, giving pilots insufficient room to build speed for a takeoff with a tail wind. The aircraft of the day also had great difficulty taking off with a cross wind, making north-south operations hazardous any time a west wind exceeded a few miles an hour.

Beachey was undoubtedly the star of the show; with his powerful custom Curtiss biplane he won more prize money than any other aviator using a single aircraft, although Sopwith was the largest individual money winner. Beachey set a world altitude record of 11,642 feet on the last day of the meet,[5] breaking the French-held international record of 11,152 and establishing a mark that would not be broken for three years. The way in which he did it was typical of his daredevil flying practices.

Concerned that the limited capacity of the fuel tank on his airplane meant that his fuel supply would be insufficient to get him high enough to set a record and return to earth, Beachey decided to use his entire supply to attain the record altitude, then attempt to glide down. His fuel lasted an hour and forty-eight minutes and took him more than two miles above the ground before the engine coughed a few times and stopped. It took him just twelve minutes to glide to a safe landing in Grant Park. Two days earlier, Parmalee, a member of the Wright team, had set an American altitude record of 10,837 feet, also eclipsed by the Beachey flight of August 20.

Two other world records were set in the meet—one a tie by Sopwith and Simon for climbing, and the other by the Wright team for duration flying. Sopwith and Simon, flying planes built by Frenchman Louis Bleriot, climbed 1,634 feet in three minutes and twenty-five seconds. G. W. Beatty set the duration record the same day by carrying a passenger in his biplane for three hours and thirty-eight minutes. Ten American records were also set in the meet, five by Sopwith.

38

Lincoln Beachey, because of his daredevil antics, was probably the most famous pilot of his time in the United States. (CHICAGO HISTORICAL SOCIETY)

The Wright Company won $16,029, in addition to $100-per-day royalties from Rodgers, Beatty, Sopwith, O.A. Brindley, and Andrew Drew—all independent contestants who used Wright airplanes. Curtiss' team won $27,291, and the Moisant team won $8,143.

In some cases a record was set one day to be eclipsed only a day later. Coffyn set a three-man duration mark on the first day of the meet only to see Sopwith eclipse it at one hour, ten minutes, and twenty-six seconds the next day and, later that day, to see Beatty break that record with a flight of one hour, eighteen minutes, and twenty-two seconds.[6]

Sopwith was awarded $14,202 in prizes, although $100 a day of that had to be paid to the Wrights as royalty under their patent. In addition to his 70-horsepower Bleriot, Sopwith also flew a Wright plane.[7] Beachey won $11,667, and Rodgers collected $11,285 in prize money. The most unfortunate participant was L. Lewkowicz, who won only sixty cents for getting his Queen monoplane into the air for just eighteen seconds. He also received the flat $250 stipend for expenses for appearing in the show.

Although hailed in Chicago and throughout the aviation world as an outstanding success, the meet was a financial failure. Despite $145,635 in revenue from tickets, programs, and advertising, the International Aviation Meet Association lost $64,019 on the show and on November 1, 1911, assessed its guarantors $75,000. The assessment included, in addition to the operating loss, a $10,000 contingent liability in the event that IAMA lost the lawsuit the Wrights had filed during the meet.

In addition to $102,938 paid to the participating aviators in prizes and expenses, the association had spent $17,551 preparing Grant Park for the show; $37,770 for grandstands and hangars; $3,087 for bands and entertainment for the crowd; $753 for field hospitals; $20,390 in administrative expenses, primarily salaries for its staff; and $19,267 for advertising and publicity.

The cost of the extravaganza caused some dissent within the Aero Club even before the meet started. Victor Lougheed, protesting the way the meet was being handled, resigned from the Aero Club August 12— the day the meet opened. "The meet itself, under the guise of a non-profit-paying corporation, has been turned into the hands of a man with the tact of a Missouri mule, whose only claim to the special knowledge desirable for the place inheres in the fact that he has pull with the city administration and was a notorious local politician out of a job," complained Lougheed.[8] The reference was to Bernard Mullaney, former city public works commissioner appointed as general manager of the meet association.

Grover Sexton, Aero Club secretary, replied with a defense of Harold F. McCormick, not Mullaney. "Where would the International Aviation Meet Association have gotten funds if Mr. McCormick had not advanced $45,000 and put up his personal bond for the $80,000 prize money and for bonding a couple of foreign machines brought here?" Sexton asked.[9] Lougheed continued his criticism with another letter[10] charging graft, corruption, and mismanagement of the air meet. McCormick intervened and asked Lougheed to reconsider, but he refused and the club reluctantly parted ways with one of its early members.

By that time, McCormick and the club were already deeply involved in their next major project—the establishment of Chicago's first real airport.

1. Covering the meet for the *Chicago Tribune* was the newspaper's first aviation correspondent, William B. Stout, who later left the newspaper to design airplanes, including the famed Ford Trimotor.

2. Because propeller governors had not been developed for practical use at that time, the aircraft of the day had to be restrained by ground crews and chocks after the engines were started and until the pilot was ready to taxi or take off. Conversely, on landing, the pilots had to shut off the engines and coast to stops.

3. Rodgers, the nation's first transcontinental pilot, was killed in a crash April 12, 1912, near Long Beach, Cal.

4. Ely, who had been the first pilot to make a shipboard takeoff when he flew from the deck of the cruiser *U.S.S. Birmingham* on Nov. 14, 1910, was killed in a crash Oct. 14, 1914, while performing in Macon, Ga.

5. Lincoln Beachey was killed in a crash in San Francisco Bay on March 14, 1915. The engine from his airplane was later salvaged and mounted on a Partridge-Keller plane built at Cicero Field and flown by aviatrix Katherine Stinson.

6. The records set in the International Aviation Meet in Chicago Aug. 12-20, 1911, include:

International

Altitude—11,642 feet; Lincoln Beachey (Curtiss 50), Aug. 20.

Two-man duration—3:42:22.2; G. W. Beatty (Wright 30), Aug. 19.

Climbing Speed—500 meters in 0:03:25; T.O.M. Sopwith (Bleriot 70), and Rene Simon (Bleriot 50), both Aug. 19.

United States

Altitude—11,642; Beachey.

Two-man Speed—0:07:50 (10 kilometers); T.O.M. Sopwith (Bleriot 70), Aug. 17 (57.785 m.p.h.)

Three-man Speed—0:06:56.4 (5 kilometers); T.O.M. Sopwith (Wright 30), Aug. 15. (54.6 m.p.h.)

Two-man Duration—3:42:22.2; Beatty.

Three-man Duration—1:18:22; G.W. Beatty (Wright 30), Aug. 13.

Climbing—500 meters in 0:03:25; Sopwith and Simon.

Weight Carrying—458 pounds; P.O. Parmelee (Wright 30), Aug. 19.

Two-Man Altitude—3,080 feet; G.W. Beatty (Wright 30), Aug. 15.

The contestants and their winnings (including each pilot's $250 stipend for expenses for appearing) in the meet include:

Pilot	Plane	Total Flying Time	Winnings
C.P. Rodgers	Wright 30	27:00:16	$11,285
G.W. Beatty	Wright 30	24:21:58	7,125
O.A. Brindley	Wright 30	23:44:54	3,351
J.J. Ward	Curtiss 50	20:36:34	3,413
A.L. Welsh	Wright 30	19:49:46	6,121
L. Beachey	Curtiss 50	14:33:05	11,667
R. Simon	Bleriot 50	9:55:47	5,050
T.O.M. Sopwith	Bleriot 70/ Wright 30	9:14:56	14,020
E. Ely	Curtiss 70	7:28:13	4,672
E.L. Ovington	Curtiss 50/ Bleriot 70	5:04:49	5,900
P.O. Parmelee	Wright 30	5:04:08	4,451
J.C. Turpin	Wright 30	4:21:07	1,022
G. Mestach	Morane 50	3:53:48	967
H.W. Hill	Wright Baby 30	3:54:17	2,450
J.A.D. McCurdy	McCurdy 50	2:55:55	2,400
J.J. Frisbie	Curtiss 50	2:49:43	2,000
J.C. Mars	Curtiss 50	2:44:08	828
J.V. Martin	Burgess Baby 50	2:38:11	750
W. Brookins	Wright 30	2:38:11	816
L. Hammond	Baldwin 80	1:51:46	1,050
P.W. Peck	Curtiss 50	1:03:53	900
A. Stone	Queen 50	1:01:28	622

F.T. Coffyn	Wright 30	0:58:56	650
H.A. Robinson	Curtiss 70	0:55:51	611
T.S. Baldwin	Baldwin 60	0:28:02	556
A. Drew	Wright 30	0:17:13	650
C.C. Witmer	Curtiss 50	0:13:38	527
L.W. Bonney	Wright 30	0:09:19	518
L. Lewkowicz	Queen 50	0:00:18	250.60
J. Cummings	Bleriot	none	250
St. Croix Johnstone	Moisant 50	4:56:36	1,093
W.R. Badger	Baldwin 60	2:28:00	900
H.N. Atwood	Burgess	unknown	1,000
Curtiss hydro-aeroplane			3,500

7. As a thank you for the winnings, Sopwith offered McCormick, from whose pocket the money for the meet had come, a free plane ride Aug. 21, the day after the meet ended.

8. Victor Lougheed letter of Aug. 12, 1911, in Aero Club files.

9. Grover Sexton letter of Aug. 18, 1911, in Aero Club files.

10. Victor Lougheed letter of Sept. 4, 1911, in Aero Club files.

Cicero Field was the center of aviation activity in Chicago during 1912. The Aero Club of Illinois sponsored weekend shows there during warm weather, and many spectators arrived on the Douglas Park rapid transit line. A Douglas train can be seen in the background just beyond the crowd. (C. R. SINCLAIR COLLECTION)

The First Airport

The 1911 air meet was perhaps Harold F. McCormick's best known accomplishment in pioneering the establishment of aviation in Chicago. A more important contribution was Cicero Field, the airport he and members of the Aero Club of Illinois developed just before the air show. For three years, Cicero Field was probably the only established airport in the Chicago area and for a time it was in all likelihood the most complete flying facility in the world. It was the site of Aero Club activities, various aeronautical manufacturing operations, some flying schools, and the place where the next generation of avaitors learned to fly.

Between Octave Chanute's glider experiments in 1896 and the 1911 air show, Chicago was something of a backwater in the development of aviation. The Wright brothers and Glenn Curtiss dominated the American aviation scene, and in Europe men such as Louis Bleriot, Gabriel and Charles Voisin, Alberto Santos-Dumont, Horatio Frederick Phillips, Henry and Maurice Farman, and Alliott Verdon Roe were largely responsible for aircraft development.

Chicago was not entirely devoid of aviation activity during the industry's first decade of existence, but the few tinkerers working in

An early attempt to build a helicopter. This one was designed and built by scenic artist James F. Scott, probably in 1910.

the city accomplished little of significance. Probably the most successful of the lot was Carl S. Bates, a mechanical engineer who built a few moderately practical flying machines. More typical of the experimenters of the day was James F. Scott, a scenic artist who became interested in aviation shortly after the Wrights first flew and in the next half decade built a succession of unsuccessful aircraft.

In January, 1908, Scott noticed an advertisement by the War Department for bids on a military airplane. Because a ten per cent deposit was required with all bids and Scott could only raise $100, he bid $1,000 to build and deliver to Fort Myer, Virginia, within 185 days a military bomber. However, he defaulted on the contract a month later when he realized his bid was far too low and he could not raise additional money to build the plane.[1] Scott finally built a multiplane with five sets of wings in 1909, although there is no record that it ever flew, and in the next year built a helicopter that was supposed to be propelled by sixteen discs. It failed to fly.

Balloonist Horace B. Wild, a notorious braggart, boasted of having built several successful airplanes, but there is no corroboration of this. Wild, Scott, Bates, and Ray Harroun—a race driver who built airplane engines—were members of a clique whose aviation activities for a while centered around the White City Amusement Park, 63rd Street and South Park Avenue.[2] The principal investor in the park, Joseph Beifeld, encouraged the use of a large building there for ballooning and had a large field nearby leveled to permit flying operations by heavier-than-air machines.

By 1910, there was also a flying field established at 65th Street and Major Avenue, just southwest of the later site of Midway Airport. Although there was never more than a handful of planes stationed there, including the Curtiss machine owned by James E. Plew. Benjamin B. Lipsner, the man who later organized the U.S. Air Mail Service, and famed pilot R. W. (Shorty) Schroeder got their starts in aviation there.

It was also the flying field used by Otto Brodie, Chicago's first pilot. Brodie, a native of Cheboygan, Wisconsin, who had been hired by Plew as a demonstration driver for White automobiles, was sent by Plew to Glenn Curtiss' factory in Hammondsport, New York, in late 1909 to learn how to fly after Plew also became the Curtiss dealer in

Chicago. Brodie then became the demonstrator for the single plane that Plew bought from Curtiss. Schroeder was his mechanic.

As early as 1907, aviation enthusiasts had organized the Aeronautique Club of Chicago with balloonist Charles E. Coey as president. The club accomplished little except the organization of the 1908 balloon race. Those early enthusiasts, with the exception of Chanute, were not wealthy men, so that the one ingredient lacking in their attempts to develop flying machines was sufficient capital. Until McCormick and Charles Dickinson came on the scene in 1910 and invested considerable sums in establishing aviation at Cicero Field, there were few ways that men of modest means could enter aviation.[3]

There was little doubt that the public was enthusiastic about flying; the 1908 balloon race and 1909 Curtiss exhibition attracted large crowds, as did the 1910 demonstration of flying by Eugene Ely and J.C. (Bud) Mars at Hawthorne Race Track. About 25,000 persons watched them perform after the regularly scheduled motorcycle races.

That crowd was small compared with the throng of 200,000 that watched in Grant Park as a twenty-two-year-old pilot, Walter P. Brookins, made the first confirmed flight over Chicago. Previous flights had all been made in the suburbs. Brookins, the first American taught to fly by the Wrights, made a number of flights September 27, 1910, to tune up for an attempt to win $10,000 offered by H.H. Kohlsaat, publisher of the *Chicago Record Herald*, for a flight between Chicago and Springfield. On September 28, Brookins carried a *Record Herald* reporter, Grover Sexton, on a seven-minute flight over Grant Park as he continued to practice for the Springfield run. "It was a pleasant experience, more like riding in an automobile on a perfectly smooth road than anything else I can think of," Sexton said after alighting. "The earth just seemed to drop out from under us. I wasn't frightened, although it was my first trip."[4]

The next day, Brookins took off from Washington Park Meadows in an attempt to set the world distance record and collect the $10,000. His destination was the State Fairgrounds in Springfield. The flight was considered important enough to warrant the presence of Wilbur Wright, who came from Dayton to watch. The flight plan called for Brookins to follow the Illinois Central Railroad right-of-way to Springfield, because in those days before highways and aerial navi-

One of Cicero's most popular pilots was "The Smiling Irishman"
Mickey McGuire. This photograph of McGuire and his mechanic,
Shorty Schroeder (rear), was taken in 1912. McGuire left Chicago the
following year and was killed in Mexico. (C. R. SINCLAIR COLLECTION)

gation aids, following the railroads was the only method of navigation available to pilots. A special car for newsmen and dignitaries had been added to the IC train to Springfield that day, and it was expected that the train would arrive before Brookins so that the passengers could watch his landing. Brookins took off at 9:15 a.m. and, despite fuel stops in Gilman and Mount Pulaski, arrived in Springfield in seven hours and ten minutes—ten minutes before the train.

A few days later (October 1), many of the nation's top aviators came to Chicago to compete in what was to be the greatest aerial extravaganza to that date—an air race to New York City. The *Chicago Evening Post* had offered $25,000 in prizes, to which Clifford Harmon, of New York, had added $5,000. The money drew the best pilots in American aviation, including Augustus Post, secretary of the Aero Club of America; Miss Blanche Scott, who was expected to be the first woman to fly over Chicago (she didn't because of high winds); Glenn Curtiss; Charles K. Hamilton; Charles F. Willard; Ely; and J.A.D. McCurdy. Unfortunately, the race turned into a fiasco even before the first plane was to take off.

Bickering among the participants and the fact that none had made a cross country trip of that length caused the race sponsors to have second thoughts. Finally, the organizers of the meet decided to pick the best pilot and plane available to make a solo attempt, and Ely was selected. Special arrangements had been made to guide him along the route. Huge white cloths with black arrows painted on them had been spread in farm fields in Indiana, and the roofs of several cars in a special railroad train that would accompany him were painted white so he could easily identify them from the air. Ely was to fly first to LaPorte, Indiana, where a large crowd awaited him on the county fairgrounds, then to South Bend, Indiana, where he was to land on a golf course. He would stay in South Bend for the night before continuing on his trip the next day.

Ely, in a fancy yellow French flying suit, took off in front of a large crowd at Hawthorne Race Track at 4:10 p.m. October 9. With a 25-mile-an-hour wind at his back, he expected to make LaPorte in record time. However, his engine quit fifteen minutes after takeoff and he was forced to land in a field at 85th Street and South Honore Avenue, a few miles from where he had taken off. Attempts were

Walter Brookins' Wright *Flyer* in Grant Park, September, 1910, prior
to his record flight to Springfield, Ill. The Art Institute can be seen in
the right background. (CHICAGO HISTORICAL SOCIETY)

made over the next few days to repair the engine and continue the flight, but mechanical problems and high winds eventually forced its cancellation.

By 1911, Chicago was in much better shape to organize a major air meet. Not only had the Aero Club managed to draw into one organization the city's aviation enthusiasts, but McCormick's wealth and prestige made it possible to plan and develop aviation activities on a grand scale. Although that capital greatly benefitted the aviation community and Aero Club, McCormick was never able to use it to develop a commercial venture.

His first attempt was in 1911, when he made a stab at designing an airplane. It was to be a revolutionary design—one that could best be described as a circular flying wing that looked something like a giant umbrella. Possibly because he was concerned about potential ridicule, he went to a field he owned in Cicero in the wee hours of the morning of July 2, 1911, to test fly it.[5]

McCormick managed to get the aircraft into the air for a few glides the length of the field, but it reportedly proved to be too difficult to turn for practical aerial operation and he ordered it disposed of after another year and a half of work failed to correct the problems. McCormick apparently was quite embarrassed by the flying umbrella, for when Percy Noel, editor of *Aero Magazine* in St. Louis, wrote to the Aero Club of Illinois for a photograph of the machine, the club's secretary and McCormick's friend, Grover Sexton, replied: "The only way I know of that I could get a picture of Mr. McCormick in his machine would be to chloroform him and call out the National Guard."[6]

McCormick's motorized umbrella may have been the first plane to fly from Cicero Field, Chicago's first real airport. Until then, all flights had been conducted from race tracks or parks at which large crowds could be accommodated or from a small number of temporary flying fields that offered little more than flat open spaces from which airplanes could take off or land.

Aero Club members had been aware that for aviation to develop in Chicago, a permanent installation was needed at which pilots could not only practice, but new pilots could learn to fly, airplanes could be built and repaired, and shows could be held. Sometime in 1911, while

Harold F. McCormick's umbrella plane was not one of the most successful aircraft. Although it was flown 12 times on May 25, 1912, by Andrew Drew, Cicero Field manager, it proved difficult to turn. (C. R. SINCLAIR COLLECTION)

the Aero Club was busily planning the impending air show, McCormick offered it 180 vacant acres he owned in west suburban Cicero for use as an airport. The site was bounded by 16th Street, 22nd Street, 48th Avenue, and 52nd Avenue. The field was ideal for flying; it was bounded on three sides by low buildings and on the fourth by the Douglas Park rapid transit line, which ran at grade level next to the field. The Metropolitan Elevated Railroad, owner of the Douglas line, even built a new station to serve the airport. The fare to downtown Chicago was five cents.

The new airport was formally opened July 4—two days after the McCormick flight in his motorized umbrella—with an exhibition of flying by several amateurs and a balloon ascension. By opening day, fifteen planes were stationed there permanently, and Aero Club members boasted that the field had a 1,500-foot runway that was 700 feet wide—"perfect for testing machines."[7] The field also had room to seat 40,000 spectators as well as space for hangars for 250 airplanes.

The four amateur pilots who shared the prize money opening day were Dan Kreamer, H.W. Powers, Otto W. Brodie, and Allan Lougheed, brother of Victor and founder of Lockheed Aircraft Company. About a week later, Kreamer became the Chicago area's first aviation fatality when his plane crashed in Cicero while he was attempting to pass his pilot licensing examination.[8] The accident occurred at 7:18 p.m. July 13, 1911, when Kreamer put his Curtiss biplane, owned by Plew, into a sharp turn at 100 feet and spun to the ground. He was taken to St. Anthony de Padua Hospital where he died at 8:40 p.m., leaving a widow and two children. The crash, coming less than a month before the 1911 air show, received front page treatment in the newspapers the next day.[9]

Despite the fatality and impending air show, Cicero Field became a beehive of activity for the remainder of July. Among the young aviators who learned to fly there that month was Harold (Kiddy) Karr, a Crane Technical High School student who tried to teach himself to fly by being pulled in a glider behind an automobile. He later went on to become the first licensed pilot in the United States Navy. A new aircraft firm, National Aeroplane Company, opened a flying school in Cicero that month.

At the conclusion of the 1911 air show, all aviation activity in the

54

Typical of the strange-looking planes that never flew in the early days
of aviation was this "tandem" aircraft built by Dan Kaiser in 1912.
Kaiser later became an air mail pilot. (C. R. SINCLAIR COLLECTION)

city moved to Cicero Field—hangars, pilots, ground crews, and airplanes. Among the first to sign agreements to use Cicero and waivers of liability for the Aero Club were C.P. Rodgers (August 24) and Dickinson (August 26). Dickinson, one of the founders of the Aero Club, was to succeed McCormick as the guiding figure in Chicago aviation.

1. The War Department had little interest in the military possibilities of the Wright brothers' new invention, despite attempts by the Wrights to generate government involvement in aviation. It was not until 1907 that the War Department, largely as a result of political pressure and the interest shown by European governments in airplanes, indicated it was willing to negotiate with the Wrights.

2. Bates, who had only modest success in aviation, was bought out in 1912 by Edward B. Heath, whose E.B. Heath Aerial Vehicle Company, organized in 1909, subsisted mainly by manufacturing aircraft parts sold primarily to builders of homemade planes. After acquiring Bates' company, Heath manufactured complete aircraft for private and commercial use until 1931.

3. One such man of modest means who for a time was successful in aviation was James E. Plew, second president of the Aero Club. However, Plew's involvement was in selling Curtiss planes from his White automobile dealership, not manufacturing or designing them. His first plane, delivered in December of 1909, was flown by Brodie.

4. *Chicago Tribune*, Sept. 29, 1910.

5. *Chicago Tribune*, July 3, 1911.

6. Grover Sexton letter of July 17, 1911, in Aero Club files.

7. *Aeronautics Magazine*, August, 1911.

8. In those days, the Aero Club, not the federal government, licensed pilots.

9. Aero Club report of July 14, 1911, in Aero Club files, and *Chicago Tribune* of the same date.

C. R. Sinclair in one of Max Lillie's Wright *Flyers* in 1912. He became active in aviation in 1910 at the flying field at 65th Street and Major Avenue used by Otto Brodie and Shorty Schroeder. (C. R. SINCLAIR COLLECTION)

Katherine Stinson was the first woman to learn to fly in Chicago. She enrolled in the Max Lillie Flying School at Cicero Field in the spring of 1912 and was awarded her pilot's license in July. She became the first woman to loop the loop and was world famous as a flyer before ill health forced her to give up flying right after World War I. (C. R. SINCLAIR COLLECTION)

1912—The Gordon Bennett Race

The Aero Club of Illinois, elated by the successes of 1911, began 1912 with the hope that it would be even more spectacular. Not only had Chicago with Aero Club sponsorship been selected that year as the site of the coveted Gordon Bennett Race—an annual international speed race—but another major international air show was planned, and Cicero Field was booming. In the two years that the Aero Club had been in existence, it had transformed Chicago from an aviation backwater into one of the international capitals of the new flying machine.

If 1912 did not live up to expectations for the Aero Club, it was probably because 1911 had been too successful. Neither the Gordon Bennett Race nor the international air show of 1912 matched the 1911 extravaganza in importance. But by the end of 1912 it was obvious that aviation in Chicago was on a sound and growing footing. The Aero Club would no longer have to nurture Chicago aviation like a newborn lamb; an irreversible momentum had been established.

Would-be aviators were flocking to Cicero Field from around the country to train at what was undoubtedly one of the nation's two or three best flight schools,[1] and the Aero Club had instituted a strong safety program. An aircraft manufacturing operation had been established at Cicero Field, and there was a successful, if limited, demonstration of the possibility of air mail service, although such service would not become a practical reality until after World War I.

The year began with Harold F. McCormick succeeding James Plew as president of the Aero Club and taking over the planning for the Bennett and international air meets. The club had applied as early as July 8, 1911, to be the site of the Bennett Race.[2] The United States was to be the host nation for the 1912 race because tradition dictated that the country that won the race each year was to be the host the next year. The 1911 race, in Eastchurch, England, had been won by American C. T. Weymann.

The Illinois club had already done considerable planning for the September 9 Bennett Race when the Aero Club of America on May 25, 1912, officially announced that Chicago would be the site. By then, the Illinois club had been in negotiations with the Wright brothers for nearly a month over the revived issue of patent royalties; Charles Dickinson had been selected to head the fund raising committee; and McCormick had begun to solicit financial support for the race from the city's business community.

As had been the case in 1911, the Wright Company[3] threatened to sue to prevent any infringement on its patents.[4] The issue was finally resolved September 7, two days before the Bennett Race was held, when the Aero Club and International Aviation Meet Association agreed to pay Orville Wright $6,000 in royalties to allow the September 12-21 international air show to proceed as scheduled. The Bennett Race was not mentioned in the settlement, but Wright had agreed not to challenge it so long as the royalties were paid on the international meet.

An unexpected development threatened the success of both events when the Aero Club of America on July 16 suspended eight of the more prominent fliers in the country for participating in an unsanctioned meet in Boston. The pilots were Lincoln Beachey, Charles K. Hamilton, Phillips W. Page, Glenn L. Martin, Paul Peck, T.J. Terrill, Farnum Fish, and Arch Freeman. The Illinois club appealed to the Aero Club of America to lift the suspensions in time for the Chicago meets, and the national organization complied August 30.

The Bennett Race was a problem for the Aero Club of Illinois almost from the start. The club had great difficulty in obtaining a plane and pilot to represent the United States against the favored French entries, had to settle for a second-rate site for the race, and was unable to induce Great Britain to send an entry. Perhaps the biggest disappointment was the withdrawal September 2 of the lone American entry because delays in obtaining the engine from France had prevented adequate testing of the machine. The withdrawal was a bitter disappointment to Dickinson, who headed the group that had financed the $17,500 airplane.

One of the problems was that the club had gotten a late start. It wasn't until April 20—less than five months before the race—that the club announced that a contest would be held to design a 115-mile-an-hour monoplane to defend America's title. The club ultimately settled on a Burgess-Curtiss airframe powered by a 160-horsepower Gnome engine, but the engine was delayed in delivery from France, which meant that it could not be fitted to the airframe in time for adequate testing.

Earlier attempts to obtain a pilot for the machine had also run into difficulty. The club approached Earl L. Ovington on July 5, but he had given up flying. The club then wired Beachey to see whether he would fly it, but his availability was clouded by his suspension. Ultimately Dickinson picked as the pilot Norman Prince, who had submitted the winning design for the aircraft,[5] although the Aero Club of America had selected another crew. The plane was scratched from the race after the two aero clubs were unable to reconcile their differences over the pilot, although the official reason given for the withdrawal was that the plane had been delivered too late for adequate testing.

The site selection process also caused problems. Grant Park, on the lakefront, was out of the question because the race had to be held over land, and Cicero Field apparently was not acceptable because 180 acres was too small. Ultimately the club selected a square-mile site in the Clearing area south of 63rd Street and east of Harlem Avenue.[6] Only a few hundred persons, mainly aviators, Aero Club members, and newsmen, were on hand when the race began at 9:38 a.m. September 9, and when it ended, there were only about 5,000 spectators—an exceptionally small crowd for such an important event.

America Defender, the United States' ill-fated entry in the 1912 Bennett race, never flew. It was scratched from the race for safety reasons. (CHICAGO HISTORICAL SOCIETY)

The withdrawal of the American entry and the failure of the British to send a contestant left the French unopposed. The race, between French pilots, was won by Jules Vedrines in a Deperdussin monoplane built especially for the race and powered by a 140-horsepower Gnome engine. He won the 124.3-mile race narrowly, flying the thirty laps in one hour, ten minutes, and fifty-six seconds—an average speed of 105.5 miles an hour.

The 1912 International Aviation Meet, which began September 12 in Grant Park,[7] again drew crowds estimated as high as 100,000 persons, but it was considered by many to be far less spectacular than the show the year before. The Aero Club in 1912 offered only $24,000 in prizes, less than a quarter of what was paid in 1911, but still managed to attract some well-known pilots. Beachey again thrilled the crowds with his aerial antics.

However, the 1912 show did top its predecessor in one respect; there were more Chicago pilots entered. In 1911, only one pilot, the ill-fated St. Croix Johnstone, was from Chicago, but the next year no fewer than sixteen of the forty-one registered pilots were Chicago residents, products of the city's aviation community, or fliers who made the city their base of operations.

Although a number of pilots had learned to fly at Cicero Field the previous year, the first formal flight training school opened there in March, 1912, under the direction of Max Lillie (ne Maximilian Theodore Liljestrant). For the eighteen months it was open, the Swedish-born Lillie turned out many new pilots who would later become famous. By mid 1913, the school had become so well known that Lillie was forced to hire instructors to keep pace with the demand for flying lessons.[8] However, the school closed after Lillie was killed September 15, 1913, while performing in Galesburg, Illinois.

One of his first students in 1912 was aviatrix Katherine Stinson, who came to Chicago from her native Mississippi at age 21 to take up flying and who, before her brief aviation career was cut short in that decade, thrilled thousands at air shows in the United States, Canada, and the Far East. She began flying lessons in March, applied for her pilot's license May 24, and passed her flight tests July 19.

Business was so good at Cicero Field in 1912 that the Aero Club on May 4 hired pilot Andrew Drew[9] to manage the place—the first airport manager in the city's history. He was paid $40 a week, and by May 14 he reported that Cicero Field had the busiest day in its brief existence with twenty-seven flights. The airport made $36.75 that week and needed additional help to control gate crashers, Drew reported. "A number of people got in without paying," he noted in his weekly report.

By August, Grover Sexton was able to boast that Cicero Field was the world's busiest airport. Since May 4, when Drew took over, Cicero had been the site of 359 flights—"more than almost all the other American fields together."[10]

There also occurred in May, 1912, several flights which, although they were not particularly notable for their success, demonstrated commercial possibilities for the day when more efficient machines were to become available. The first occurred May 25, when 18-year-old pilot Farnum Fish flew from Cicero to Milwaukee carrying four bolts of silk and 7,500 handbills advertising the Boston Store. Fish dumped the leaflets over Milwaukee, then ran out of gas and landed in a park after a two-hour-and-six-minute flight. The 90-mile flight was probably the longest over water flight to that time.[11]

Five days later, Lillie and several associates conducted one of the many demonstrations of the possibility of air mail that the U.S. Post Office Department had arranged around the country. The initial air mail flight was almost an accident. Lillie and Miss Stinson had gotten lost returning to Cicero Field and instead set down in a farm field near Elmhurst, where the local postmaster, thinking that the demonstration flight was to begin a day ahead of schedule, gave him a sack of mail to fly back to Chicago. The next day he flew back to Elmhurst with eighty pounds of mail, and on June 2, pilots Paul Studenski and Marcel Tournier flew mail between Cicero, Elmhurst, and Wheaton. A total of 458 pounds of mail was flown during the four-day demonstration program.

Meanwhile, the Aero Club continued to license pilots receiving their training at Cicero Field. Besides Drew, among those receiving training the first year of the airport's existence were several aviators who went on to fame in their new profession—Glenn L. Martin, founder of the company bearing his name, which eventually built 12,000 airplanes before dropping them in favor of aerospace work;

Norman Prince, one of the founders of the famed Lafayette Escadrille of World War I; and Chauncey (Chance) M. Vought, founder of the company bearing his name, which later built military aircraft.

Cicero Field's record was marred by two fatal crashes that year, both of them connected with the 1912 international meet. Paul Peck was killed September 11 while testing his plane, and Howard Gill died as a result of the city's first mid-air collision. It occurred September 14, when a plane being flown by Belgian pilot George Mestach overtook and hit another, flown by Gill, in the tail. Mestach survived, but Gill died of injuries en route to the hospital.[12]

Despite what seems today like an extraordinarily high number of crashes in those early years of aviation, flying was not unduly dangerous, considering the technical state of the art. And by 1912 the aviation community had in place a regulatory system to insure that flying was as safe as possible. The problem was that the official aviation organizations could not enforce their regulations on anyone who chose to ignore them.

Octave Chanute was probably the first to acknowledge publicly the consideration of safety when, in 1896, he chose the Indiana dunes for his experiments because the sand and water made it less likely that his associates would be hurt in a crash. However, for about a decade after the Wrights first built their machine, the problem of safety was solely the concern of the pilot or aircraft manufacturer. Because airplanes were light, slow, and few in number in those early years, the first aviation fatality was not recorded until September 17, 1908, when Army Lieutenant Thomas Selfridge was killed in the crash of a plane being demonstrated at Fort Myer by Orville Wright.

The organizations that had been formed to promote aviation decided soon thereafter that some measure of safety regulation was needed. The members of the Federation Aeronautique Internationale, the worldwide aviation organization of its day, meeting in October, 1910, in Paris, adopted the industry's first formal standards, including the licensing of airplane, balloon, and dirigible pilots. The individual licensing in each country was left to the FAI affiliate there—the Aero Club of America in the case of the United States.

However, FAI regulations spelled out that anyone receiving a pilot's license would have to be at least 18 years old and pass a series of

Katherine Stinson taking off from Cicero Field in her Chicago-built Partridge-Keller *Looper*. (E. M. LAIRD COLLECTION)

tests—including twice flying a five-kilometer closed circuit, climbing to a minimum altitude of fifty meters, successfully negotiating a figure eight, landing within fifty meters of a predesignated point, and turning off the engine before touching down. The FAI, which printed the regulations in six languages of its sixteen member nations, forwarded an English copy of them to the Aero Club of America with the notation that they would become effective February 15, 1911. The Aero Club of America delegated to the Aero Club of Illinois the authority to conduct the required tests for prospective pilots, although the licenses would be issued by the national organization. The first FAI pilot's license in America was issued to Glenn Curtiss June 8, 1911.

Unfortunately, the aviation organizations had no way of preventing unlicensed pilots from flying, although they could be excluded from sanctioned events. The aviation clubs also had no power to regulate the safe construction of flying machines; anyone could build an airplane in his back yard and attempt to fly it. Federal licensing of pilots and aircraft did not begin until 1926.

Nevertheless, the various aviation organizations from 1911 took steps to insure that flying was as safe as possible. The Aero Club of Illinois on August 11, 1911, turned down a request by a couple to have an airborne wedding performed at the international meet that year and vetoed an earlier suggestion that a plane take off from the deck of a lake steamer at the show.[13] G. F. Campbell Wood, an official of the Aero Club of America, on June 13 expressed strong reservations about the safety of some of the events proposed for the 1911 Chicago show. He warned that the course planned for speed races carried the airplanes too close to the area reserved for the crowd: "The flyers themselves participating in the meet on a small circuit, of course, more or less take their life (sic) in their hands: that is their lookout, but the spectators should be protected to the limit." The course was modified at his suggestion.

1. The Cicero Field flight school was not the city's first. The Chicago School of Aviation opened for business in April, 1911, to train pilots at a modest flying field at 118th Street and Morgan Avenue, but fell into bankruptcy in thirteen months. Apparently the relatively remote location, compared with

that of Cicero Field, which was on a transit line, contributed to its failure.

2. Grover Sexton's letter of July 8, 1911, to G.F. Campbell Wood, secretary of the Aero Club of America, in Aero Club files.

The Gordon Bennett races were held five times before being suspended because of World War I. The races were named for *New York Herald* publisher James Gordon Bennett Jr., an early aviation racing and balloon enthusiast and promoter. The dates, locations, course, time, and winners of the five Bennett races were:

Aug. 28, 1909; Rheims, France; 20 kilometers; 15:50.4; Glenn Curtiss, USA.

Oct. 29, 1910; Belmont Park, N.Y.; 62 miles; 1:01:04.7; Claude Graham-White, UK.

July 1, 1911; Eastchurch, England; 94 miles; 1:11:36.2; C.T. Weyman, USA.

Sept. 9, 1912; Chicago, Ill.; 124.3 miles; 1:10:58.85; Jules Vedrines, France.

Sept. 29, 1913; Rheims, France; 200 kilometers; 59:45.6; Maurice Prevost, France.

3. Wilbur Wright died May 30, 1912, of typhoid fever in Dayton, Ohio.

4. Norman Prince letter of Aug. 3, 1912, in Aero Club files.

5. Prince's selection by Dickinson caused a dispute that may have been the most important factor in the withdrawal of the plane from the race. The Aero Club of America had designated as the U.S. team Glenn Martin, DeLloyd Thompson, and Paul Peck, and as alternates, Howard Gill and Max Lillie. Dickinson, reminding everyone that he had invested $17,500 in the airplane, disputed the national organization's selections and withdrew the aircraft from the race.

6. This race course, as well as the one used in the 1911 international meet, was designed by James S. Stephens, a Chicago engineer and Aero Club member.

7. Cicero Field was also used during the meet for some activities, although it was used mainly as a logistical and maintenance base and a practice field.

8. Among the instructors hired by Lillie was pilot DeLloyd Thompson.

9. Drew was killed June 12, 1913, when he crashed the famed airplane *VinFiz* during an exhibition in Lima, Ohio.

10. Aero Club of America Bulletin, August, 1912.

11. Although Farnum Fish's flight at 90 miles was considered an over water record, it was made entirely within sight of and parallel to the lakeshore. Frenchman Louis Bleriot made the first significant over water flight in a heavier-than-air machine when he crossed the English Channel on July 25, 1909, and Logan (Jack) Vilas was the first to cross Lake Michigan when he flew 64 miles between St. Joseph, Mich., and Chicago on July 1, 1913.

12. Julia Clark became the first woman aviator to die in a crash when her plane went down June 17, 1912, while she was performing in Springfield, Ill.

Mrs. Clark, the first woman graduate of Curtiss' San Diego school a few months earlier, came to Chicago shortly before the fatal incident and was warned by Drew at Cicero Field not to fly in the Springfield show because she did not have enough experience. Aero Club officials said she rejected the advice after being induced to fly by an "anxious promoter."

13. Some of the ideas to promote safety in 1912 now sound somewhat amusing. Ole Flattorp, who built most of the aircraft propellers in use at Cicero Field, suggested on March 14, 1912, to the Aero Club that it equip a special transit car to be used on the Douglas Park line adjacent to Cicero Field to test propellers. He suggested that the car be equipped with instruments to measure thrust, revolutions per minute, the speed of the car, and power used to operate the propeller. There is no record of the idea having been adopted, although testing propellers on a train would have been inherently safer than testing them in flight.

Planes at Ashburn were refueled from underground tanks. This military DH-4 is being positioned over the fuel box (on ground near the wheels). (ALFRED O. SPORRER COLLECTION)

Ashburn Field

By the time the United States entered World War I in 1917, the Aero Club of Illinois had firmly established aviation in Chicago, but the organization's absolute authority over the young industry was noticeably diminished. The club still ran the only real airport in Chicago and put on the best air shows, but aviation had grown to the point where it could no longer be controlled by a single organization.

The club itself had lost some of its pioneering zeal. Harold F. McCormick had faded from the scene to be replaced as president of the Aero Club by Charles Dickinson, who in 1916 financed the development of a new airport—Ashburn Field. The war in Europe also had a profound influence, although it was thousands of miles away; European aviators and machines were no longer available for U.S. air shows. The war forced the cancellation of the 1914 Gordon Bennett Race and with it the United States' chance to recapture the title it lost to France in Chicago and which was retained by the French in 1913 in Rheims.

Despite the problems, the Aero Club still managed to sponsor, promote, and participate in several aerial shows that continued to draw large crowds in Chicago, even though aviation was no longer the novelty it had been in 1911. After all, anyone in Chicago wanting to see flying machines after 1911 had only to drive or take the Douglas Park train to Cicero Field on the weekend. However, most of the major flying shows continued to be held in Grant Park to attract large crowds. In fact, Grant Park remained a major site of Chicago aviation events through World War I and into the 1920s, although a permanent airport was not established there until 1919 when the U.S. Air Mail Service began operations. Nevertheless, its location adjacent to the central business district of a major American city resulted in its being the site of a number of significant aviation events, including the record flights of Walter Brookins to Springfield in 1910, Harry Atwood between St. Louis and New York in 1911, Ruth Bancroft Law to New York in 1916, and Katherine Stinson to New York with a load of mail in 1918.

As important as those flights were to aviation purists, the crowds in Chicago much preferred the spectacular Grant Park air shows, and because of the park's convenience to public transportation, Chicago residents turned out by thousands to watch daredevils like Lincoln Beachey perform. In various shows between 1911 and his death in 1915, Beachey did things like swooping low over Michigan Avenue buildings to force the spectators on the roofs to duck. He also dressed as a woman and flew just over the tops of automobiles on Michigan Avenue, causing some Chicago area residents to grumble that women should not be allowed to fly. Beachey made his last Chicago appearance during the May 16-18, 1914 air show.

He was not the only daredevil to perform in Grant Park, however, Art (Smash Up) Smith, sometimes known as the "Boy Aviator", entertained large crowds March 9, 1915, with various flying stunts, including a night exhibition of looping the loop with twenty four Roman candles attached to his Curtiss biplane. The newspaper reporters of the day were properly impressed: "Smith shot up from Grant Park with a whirl and a flash of light that made his machine look like a fireworks factory," a *Tribune* reporter said.[1]

Later the same year, other Chicago-based aviators, including Katherine Stinson and Emil (Matty) Laird, drew large crowds to Grant Park for a six-day aerial carnival, although the attention of the press by that time had been diverted because of the steamship *Eastland*

Art "Smash Up" Smith was something of a wag in the air and on the ground. He was one of the better stunt pilots and daredevils at Cicero Field, and went on to become a respected air mail pilot before his death in a crash on Feb. 12, 1926. (UNITED AIRLINES)

Harold F. McCormick's Curtiss flying boat being tested at Hammondsport, N.Y. in 1914. (GLENN CURTISS MUSEUM)

disaster a few weeks before.[2] Nevertheless, Laird made aviation history at the aerial carnival August 2-7 by becoming the first person to loop the loop with a passenger, Katherine Stinson's sister, Marjorie.

During World War I, a number of air shows were held in the park to solicit support for the war effort. Ruth Law returned to Chicago in July, 1917, and dropped enlistment "bombs" on a crowd watching a military parade. On September 4, 1918, military pilots from Chanute put on a mock air battle over the park as part of a week-long war exposition.

That same day, the U.S. Post Office Department announced that the park had been selected as the site for the Air Mail Service's Chicago airport. Regularly scheduled service to Grant Park began the following year and lasted into 1920. By that time, the Post Office bowed to pressure from the Chicago business community and moved its Chicago terminal to the western suburbs. Chicagoans apparently were willing to have occasional shows staged in the park but did not want it used as a permanent airport, disrupting other activities scheduled there.

The lakefront area along Grant Park was also the site of a seaplane craze that affected many Aero Club members.

As early as 1913, McCormick's interest in land-based aviation, which had been the Aero Club's staple to that time, began to diminish and he turned his attention to hydroplanes, or flying boats. Although he was succeeded in 1913 as Aero Club president by Bion J. Arnold, an engineer and transportation planner, his influence was still sufficient to make seaplanes the dominant preoccupation of the club that year despite the fact that at that time they could be no more than a rich man's toy. On March 18 of that year, the club, at McCormick's urging, agreed to sponsor jointly, with an aviation magazine, a hydroplane race off Grant Park.[3] A hydroplane meet had been held September 17-21, 1912, along the Chicago lakefront as part of the Aero Club's international air show that year, but it was decided that the 1913 show would be devoted entirely to flying boats.

An Aero Club dinner was held April 12, 1913, to plan for establishing a "hydroaerodrome," complete with a permanent clubhouse, bungalows for resident pilots, and hangars. The facility was never built, although there was considerable hydroplane flying

75

Glenn L. Martin with his hydroplane after being forced down near
Muskegon, Mich., in the 1913 Great Lakes Reliability Race. (C. R.
SINCLAIR COLLECTION)

from the area of Clarendon Beach on Chicago's North Side, and McCormick ultimately established a private seaplane base in Lake Forest.

McCormick purchased his first hydroplane in May, 1913, from Glenn Curtiss, announcing his intention to use it to commute from his home to his office in downtown Chicago. About the same time, another wealthy Chicagoan, Logan A. (Jack) Vilas, bought a similar machine from Curtiss. The McCormick seaplane—a tractor type[4] powered by a 100-horsepower engine and with a range of approximately 400 miles—was short lived; it was destroyed, probably on July 15, 1913, when Max Lillie crashed it into the lake off Clarendon Beach and only the engine was salvaged. McCormick quickly bought a replacement.

The Aero Club's hydroplane race of 1913, officially called the "Great Lakes Reliability Tour," was originally intended to be conducted over a two-mile course within sight of Grant Park, but ultimately was expanded into an elaborate, 900-mile aerial marathon between Chicago and Detroit covering the lengths of lakes Michigan and Huron. Vilas practiced for the race July 1 by becoming the first person to fly across Lake Michigan—a 64-mile, one hour and thirty-four minute trip between St. Joseph, Michigan, and Grant Park. In fact, Vilas' journey may have been the longest over-water flight to that time; most such flights in that day were conducted entirely within sight of shore due to the unreliability of the aircraft. Thus Farnum Fish's 90-mile record "over water" flight in 1912 was never more than a few hundred feet from land.

Vilas later recounted that he lost sight of land because of a mist over Lake Michigan and was forced to navigate by watching the action of the wind against the water. He had on board a crude altimeter, but no compass. He attempted to stay at an altitude of 2,000 feet, but because of the mist and updrafts, eventually flew at 5,000 feet, an altitude that he said he was concerned his aircraft would not be able to maintain. "Frankly, I was scared. How did I know that airplane would hold together up there in that thin air?" said Vilas later.[5] However, Vilas attempted the flight with less than five hours' flight experience.[6]

The scheduled start of the Chicago to Detroit race July 5 had to be

Tony Jannus taxiing his Benoist out into the Lake from the foot of Van Buren Street in the hydroplane meet of July, 1913. Jannus went on to start the country's first air line between Tampa and St. Petersburg, Florida. (C. R. SINCLAIR COLLECTION)

postponed because of high winds, and again July 7 when Glenn Martin crashed into the lake in his seaplane just off Van Buren Street. He was not injured, however. Despite the delays, a sizeable crowd was on hand July 8 when the hydroplanes finally took off on the first leg of the race to Michigan City, Indiana, Anthony Jannus in his 75-horsepower Benoist seaplane was the first into the air, followed in rapid succession by nine of the other 11 planes. Roy Francis did not get airborne until the next day, and Martin followed July 10, after his plane was repaired.

Jannus' lead lasted only a few hours or until his plane was damaged off Gary, Indiana, forcing him out of the race. Storms over the lakes delayed the fliers further, and by July 12 only three were still in the race. When Beckwith Havens and his passenger, J.R. Verplanck, arrived in Detroit July 18, theirs was the only plane still flying. The total elapsed flying time was fifteen hours and thirty minutes, although the race had taken ten days. Havens' average speed was 60 miles an hour.[7]

The interest of McCormick and Vilas in seaplanes continued through 1913 and 1914 despite the destruction of McCormick's first machine. He bought another and hired pilot Charles C. Witmer to fly the replacement aircraft on his daily commute to Grant Park. By early 1914, McCormick, Plew, and Bion J. Arnold announced they planned to start a commuter airline using seaplanes to carry passengers between various north shore suburbs, Grant Park, and the South Shore Country Club. Lake Shore Airline, as it was named, was intended to be a profit-making venture, and passengers between Chicago and Lake Forest were charged a steep $28 for a round trip ride. The airline used two flying boats to make four daily round trips. The airline did not last long because the irregular and strong winds along the lake made a shamble of schedules.[8]

For all intents and purposes, the attempt to launch the commuter airline was McCormick's last fling in aviation. In September, 1913, he sold Cicero Field to the Grant Land Association for development, although the firm allowed the Aero Club to use the site for another two years. However, McCormick's action left the club in the awkward position of not knowing how long Cicero Field would be available, and in early 1914, James S. Stephens, first vice president of the Aero

Emil M. (Matty) Laird, then 18, flew his *Baby Biplane* at Cicero in 1913. He built the airplane himself—probably the first successful aircraft built in Chicago. (E. M. LAIRD COLLECTION)

Club, wrote the Grant Land Association to clarify the situation. The association allowed the Aero Club to continue to use the site as an airport but required that it be ready to vacate the land on twenty days' notice.[9]

In the meantime, scores of young aviators won their wings, including 18-year-old Emil (Matty) Laird, who in September, 1913, started to build his first airplane at Cicero Field. The machine was a small biplane powered by a four-cylinder, 12-horsepower, air-cooled engine, and Laird managed to get it into the air at Cicero despite warnings that a plane with such a small engine would never fly. Laird went on to found an aircraft manufacturing firm that produced airplanes into the 1930s.

Cicero was also the site of another of the many attempts to prove the feasibility of flying mail, this one sponsored by the *Chicago Tribune* October 17, 1914, between Des Moines, Iowa, and Chicago. Pilot William Robinson[10] left Des Moines with a load of mail, but flew into deteriorating weather as he neared his destination and had to divert his plane to Kentland, Indiana, to land safely. The first day's flight covered a record 390-mile distance non stop in four hours and forty-four minutes. Robinson flew to Cicero the next day.

Possibly the airport's last hurrah occurred July 18, 1915, when an Aero Club show attracted several thousand spectators to watch, among other things, Katherine Stinson loop the loop—the first time a woman did so. Her airplane, built in the Elmer Partridge and Henry Keller aircraft factory at Cicero, was powered by the engine salvaged from Lincoln Beachey's fatal wreck and purchased from his estate.

Despite the success of the show, the exodus from Cicero Field began shortly thereafter. In August of that year, Partridge and Keller moved their factory and flight school to a new field they developed on the north side of 87th Street just west of Pulaski Road. Laird remained at Cicero, however, and started work on his second plane, the Laird-Anzani 45-horsepower "Bone Shaker." It was the biplane that he and Katherine Stinson used for stunt flying for the next few years. Even while he was working on it, the Grant Land Association was making final plans to develop the airport site. On January 26, 1916, all hangars and equipment there were donated to the Aero Club, provided they move it to a new location.[11] Laird was the last to leave;

Marjorie Stinson (NATIONAL AIR AND SPACE MUSEUM)

on April 16 he flew his "Baby Biplane" to the Partridge-Keller airport, and Cicero Field ceased to exist.

Dickinson, who with McCormick's withdrawal from the aviation scene had become the Aero Club's principal patron, had already begun to look for a new airport site. In the meantime, the pilots who had used Cicero Field maintained their aircraft temporarily at the Partridge-Keller airport. On April 17, Dickinson closed the deal on 640 acres at 83rd Street and Cicero Avenue[12] to be used as the club's new airport. It was named Ashburn Field after a railroad station nearby.

Walter R. Brock, an aeronautical engineer who had won several international races in Europe, was hired to manage the airport. It was officially dedicated October 28, 1916, with a flying show featuring Marjorie Stinson and the opening of an Army aviation training facility. By December, the club had built a 75-foot-high steel tower to enable its airport manager to watch aviation activities there. Although there is no indication that it was used to control aircraft—a function of later airport towers—some aviation officials have traced the development of later control towers to that structure.

Ashburn's major drawbacks were its inaccessibility and poor drainage which made improvements expensive to build. It was served only by dirt roads and had no utilities, a serious problem when Laird was attempting to establish a major aircraft manufacturing operation in Chicago in 1925. When regular airmail service was started by the U.S. Post Office Department in 1918, Ashburn was considered so remote that the mail planes used Grant Park as their regular airport, although maintenance on the planes was performed at Ashburn. The club even built a hangar at Ashburn later in 1918 in an unsuccessful attempt to induce the Air Mail Service to relocate its operations there from Grant Park.

The club came the closest in July 18, 1919, when Bion J. Arnold set up a meeting between Aero Club members and the Chicago Aviation Commission in the Congress Hotel to present a proposal by the club to improve Ashburn Field so it could replace Grant Park. The commission, convinced that Grant Park was too limited to remain an airport, for a time seemed interested in Ashburn, but an aviation disaster in downtown Chicago a few days later doomed the idea and

Al Sporrer with his sister-in-law at Ashburn Field on May 15, 1924, after a solo flight in the Jenny behind him. Sporrer went on to become a corporate pilot and a captain for Pan American World Airways. (ALFRED O. SPORRER COLLECTION)

soured the commission on the development of aviation.

In the political furor that followed the crash of the blimp *Wingfoot Air Express* into a Loop bank, most Aero Club members backed away from the plan to expand Ashburn Field and spent their time defending aviation against its critics. The political establishment in Chicago would not again consider making a substantial financial investment in aviation facilities for another seven years. By that time, the city's principal airport was again in the western suburbs.

1. Smith, a resident of Fort Wayne, Ind., was killed Feb. 12, 1926, while flying the mail.

2. The *Eastland,* a cruise ship, capsized in the Chicago River off Dearborn Street July 24, 1915, drowning 835 persons in what is still the worst disaster in the history of the Great Lakes.

3. *Aero and Hydro Magazine,* March 22, 1913.

4. "Tractor" at the time was used to describe a front-mounted engine. The usual practice at the time was to mount the engine facing the rear.

5. *Chicago Tribune,* July 2, 1948.

6. Vilas, who died May 15, 1976, in Chicago, continued to maintain an interest in flying and yachting most of his life. He was taught to fly by Glenn Curtiss at his Hammondsport, N.Y. flying school in 1912 just before his record cross-lake flight. On June 7, 1914, Vilas conducted a successful air-sea rescue with his hydroplane after another pilot, Anthony Stadleman, crashed into the lake off Clarendon Beach. On June 22, 1915, Vilas used his seaplane to prove to Wisconsin conservation officials near Trout Lake, Wis., the feasibility of using airplanes to spot forest fires. Later, he headed the Civil Air Patrol in Illinois, and in 1942 was instrumental in obtaining membership in that organization for Miss Willa Beatrice Brown, a black woman and first member of her race in the CAP. In 1962, United Airlines honored Vilas' contributions to aviation by naming a Boeing 720 jet for him.

7. *Flying Magazine,* August, 1913.

8. McCormick speech Dec. 1, 1917, before the Pscyhology Club of Zurich, Switzerland.

9. Williard T. Block, association secretary-treasurer, in a letter of Jan. 26, 1914, in Aero Club files.

10. Robinson was killed March 11, 1916, while attempting to set an altitude record near his home town of Grinnell, Iowa.

11. McCormick letter of Jan. 24, 1916, in Aero Club files.

12. The site extended from 79th Street to 87th Street and from Cicero Avenue to Crawford Avenue, later known as Pulaski Road.

Charles Dickinson

Although he was not as well known as some of his contemporaries, Charles Dickinson probably contributed more to the development of aviation in Chicago than any other person. For the quarter century from 1910 to his death in 1935, Dickinson was a constant presence in the aviation community, financing projects that otherwise would not have been undertaken, helping barnstorming pilots down on their luck, encouraging young people to take to the air, and constantly promoting flying; yet his principal claim to fame in the newspapers of the day was that he was the nation's oldest pilot.

Dickinson's four major aviation ventures were all bitter disappointments, but after each collapsed he returned to the flying fields to try something else. After his racing plane failed to get off the ground in the 1912 Gordon Bennett Race, Dickinson turned his attention elsewhere and financed the development of Ashburn Field so that aviation in Chicago could continue to have a base of operations. When he failed to convince Chicago's political establishment to develop Ashburn as a municipal airport, he attempted to start airline service between Chicago and New York using Ashburn as a base. After that failed, he tried his hand at a government air mail contract for service between Chicago and St. Paul-Minneapolis in competition with a consortium that included some of the wealthiest and most powerful men in the city. That failed and Dickinson turned to airplane racing.

After Octave Chanute's death in 1910 and Harold F. McCormick's withdrawal from aviation five years later, it was Dickinson who used his wealth and influence to keep Chicago's fragile young aviation community alive until the development of the air mail routes in the next decade made aviation a commercially viable industry. There is no way of determining how much of his wealth he poured into aviation, but it is certain that he got very little financial return on the investment. Aviation was to Dickinson, as with Chanute, an all-encompassing avocation to which he devoted the last part of his life.

He was born May 28, 1858, the youngest of six children, in a small cottage on State Street where the Carson Pirie Scott & Company department store now stands. His father, Albert, founded the Dickinson Feed and Seed Company in 1855. It was destroyed in the Chicago Fire of 1871, but the family rebuilt it into one of the largest companies of its kind in the world. It was the success of the seed company that permitted Dickinson to invest heavily in aviation ventures.

Young Dickinson studied medicine for a while, as did his sister, Frances, who became an eye surgeon. However, Dickinson did not find medicine to his liking and instead went into the family business with his older brother. It is not known when he first developed an interest in aviation, but he was present with Chanute and McCormick on October 15, 1909, when Glenn Curtiss urged the formation of an aero club in Illinois.

His serious involvement in aviation really dates from 1910, when his wife, Marie, whom he had married in 1897, died. The next year, Dickinson sold the family house at 603 N. Dearborn St., and moved its contents[1] into a warehouse and himself into a suite in the Blackstone Hotel overlooking Grant Park. For the remaining twenty-five years of his life he lived first in the Blackstone and later in the Union League Club.

A Quaker, he neither smoked nor drank, although his associates said he was not a church-going man. He always wore identical business suits, and he operated his seed company more progressively than most businessmen of that day did. The company had a free employee cafeteria and medical department, and during hard times Dickinson gave his employees interest-free loans with which to buy homes. When his brother retired as president of the company, Dickinson assumed control with the title of vice president, leaving the title of president unfilled in deference to his brother. He disliked driving automobiles, liked train travel, and loved airplanes.

When Chanute, McCormick, James Plew, and Dickinson formed the Aero Club in 1910 to promote aviation, there was little to promote. The city had few aviators, no airports worthy of the name, and possibly one operable flying machine. McCormick and Dickinson took the train to New York City that October to watch the Belmont air show. It was there that Dickinson probably took his first plane ride, paying 1910 Gordon Bennett Race winner Claude Graham-White $500 for a ride lasting only a few minutes. The two Chicagoans were sufficiently impressed by what they saw to persuade the rest of the Aero Club upon their return to sponsor an air show in Chicago the next year. McCormick's wealth made the show possible, but Dickinson helped organize the meet as well as Aero Club activities at Cicero Field in 1911.

He was almost continuously at Cicero Field that year, and the men who remembered him there said that despite his stature as one of the city's moneyed elite, he was not afraid to get his hands dirty helping to work on a flying machine. He apparently took his first plane ride in Chicago on August 27, 1911, several days after the air show ended, when he went up with Calbraith P. Rogers.

While other Aero Club members prepared for the 1912 air show, Dickinson was given the task of finding an American entry for the Gordon Bennett Race, to be held that year in Chicago. That meant raising the money to build an airplane to represent the United States under Aero Club sponsorship, and Dickinson was plagued with trouble almost from the beginning. Because the 1911 air show lost money, Dickinson could find few persons willing to invest in a plane, which had to be designed and built from scratch to be able to compete with the more advanced European monoplanes that were expected to be entered. The Europeans, after lagging behind the U.S. in aviation for nearly a decade, had made considerable progress in building swift monoplanes for racing. Americans had concentrated mainly on the slower, but more reliable, biplanes.

After unsuccessfully soliciting for funds for the plane, Dickinson pledged his financial support to the project and on June 22—less than four months before the race was to be held—ordered a racer from the Burgess Company based on a design submitted by Norman Prince. The specifications called for an aiplane capable of flying at 115 miles an hour to compete with the French entries in the race. The engine ordered for the plane was a French Gnome.

It proved impossible to put the racer together on such short notice. The Gnome was delivered late, attached to the airframe, and hurriedly shipped to Chicago. However, it arrived only a few days before the race and had not even been test flown. Considerable bickering over the plan's airworthiness and the pilot to fly it ensued, and on September 2 Dickinson gave up and announced that, in the interest of safety, he was withdrawing it from the race.[2]

The sleek monoplane, which had been named *America Defender,* never flew. After it was displayed for a few days at Cicero Field, Dickinson had it shipped to a vacant lot behind his seed company offices at 35th Street and California Avenue, where it sat alongside several old automobiles and rotted. The *America Defender* had cost Dickinson $17,500.[3]

He shrugged off the *America Defender* fiasco and launched into several other aviation projects. One of his favorite activities was to be flown over the city, often by pilot Max Lillie, scouting for future airport sites. At the time, McCormick's interest in aviation was waning, and it was obvious to Dickinson that it was only a matter of time before the Aero Club had to find a replacement for Cicero Field. Dickinson realized that the airplane would play an important role in Chicago commerce and looked for airport sites in remote areas, away from residential development, that would provide room for expansion as aviation grew in importance. He became convinced that the Lake Calumet area on the far South Side was the perfect site for an airport and seaplane base.

In 1929, he donated 65 acres he had purchased on Lake Calumet to the city for eventual development as an airport.[4] A surprised City Council accepted the gift, but did nothing with the land. In the 1940s the Lake Calumet area was considered as one of the sites for a new jet port for the city; however, it was too remote and lost out to Orchard Place Airport on the Northwest Side, which became O'Hare International Airport.

Much of Dickinson's time in the years before World War I were spent promoting aviation. After his election as Aero Club president, he got the club to start a youth program in Chicago high schools. Matty Laird was one of the products of that program. Like many aviation pioneers, Dickinson also realized that aviation had a military application and urged Congress to form an air force.

Dickinson became preeminent in Chicago aviation in 1915 when McCormick, by then spending most of his time in Switzerland, began selling off Cicero Field to developers. Dickinson promptly bought the site for Ashburn Field and paid for the development of runways, hangars, access roads, a bunkhouse for pilots, and a well for water.[5] Once Ashburn was in operation, Dickinson tried to get the U.S. government to establish an air base there and tried to convince the city to develop it as a major airport.

That project, too, ended in failure. Although military units were twice stationed there in World War I, the government ultimately built Chanute Air Field in Rantoul, Illinois, as its major installation in northern Illinois. The city was moderately interested in the possibility of a municipal airport until the *Wingfoot Air Express* disaster in 1919. Attempts by Dickinson after World War I to interest the U.S. Post Office Department in using Ashburn as a base for its fledgling air mail service also failed, although the field was used as a maintenance facility for air mail planes using Grant Park. In the early 1920s, when the Post Office was looking for a facility to replace Grant Park, the airport chosen was Checkerboard Field in west suburban Maywood, not Ashburn.[6]

A few years later, when the commercial airlines began carrying the mail, they chose Chicago's new Municipal Airport, later renamed Midway. Ashburn continued as a general aviation field of diminishing importance until it was sold to developers in the early 1950s.[7]

By 1919, Dickinson had become interested in the possibility of establishing a commercial airline. The development of larger airplanes and more powerful engines during World War I raised the possibility

The Lawson airliner was an early attempt to build an airframe for commercial passenger service. It proved to be seriously under-powered, although it did make a flight with passengers between Ashburn Field and Washington, D.C., in 1919. (GEORGE HARDIE JR. COLLECTION)

that commercial service was feasible, although, as the early airline entrepreneurs learned, the aircraft of that time were still not sufficiently reliable to win the public's confidence.

A case in point was Dickinson's 1919 venture. Alfred W. Lawson, a Milwaukee resident, had built the first American large cabin transport. The plane, which weighed seven tons fully loaded, could carry 24 passengers, was powered by two 400-horsepower Liberty engines, and had a 94-foot wingspan. Although the aircraft was seriously underpowered,[8] Dickinson believed that it had sufficient potential for him to join Lawson in attempting to establish a passenger airline between Chicago and New York City.

The plane left Ashburn Field August 31, 1919, on the maiden revenue flight of the newly formed Lawson Airline Company with pilot Charles Cox at the controls and Chicagoan Ralph Diggins in the navigator's seat. However, when Cox arrived in Toledo on the first leg of the flight, he discovered that the designated landing field was covered with debris and was forced to try to set the plane down in a farm field. A wing struck a tree, damaging the plane, although none of the crew or eight passengers was injured. The plane was repaired and continued on to New York and Washington before returning to Milwaukee. Realizing the plane needed more power. Lawson built a three-engine version, but it crashed on its first flight in Milwaukee in May, 1921, causing his company to fail.

Undaunted, Dickinson tried again in 1923 to start an airline between Chicago and New York. On July 26, he became the first passenger to travel at night between the two cities. With pilot Eddie Stinson at the controls and mechanic Art Gray on board, Dickinson left Ashburn in a single-engine, all-metal Junkers at 11 p.m. and made Curtiss Field in Garden City, New York, at 8:30 the next morning in a flight to demonstrate the feasibility of such service. Late that year, Dickinson announced that his New York airline would begin service May 1.

"I'll probably spend a great many thousands of dollars this summer in starting this line," Dickinson said in announcing the non-stop night service. "I may never make a cent out of it, but I don't care. If I can prove that such a line can be operated from Chicago and thereby put this city on the map as a center of American aviation, I will be satisfied. I have lived 65 years now, and I have been playing with airplanes for 14 years, and my only wish is to see Chicago become the center of American flying."[9]

Nothing more was heard of the proposed airline until May 2, 1924, when Dickinson telephoned several Chicago newspapers from New York to announce that it had made its first flight. He and pilot Elmer Partridge made the maiden flight from Ashburn to Garden City in eight hours and fifteen minutes with a lunch stop in Cleveland. He told the newspapers that he and Partridge were canvassing Manhattan that night for passengers for the return trip and that the new airline had three French-built Brequets, bought from Tony Yackey, ready for service.

Unfortunately, the public was not yet ready for the rigors of flying, especially when the available alternatives were the comfortable Broadway and Twentieth Century Limited trains. The airplanes of the day were unheated and cramped. Thus Dickinson's newest venture quickly failed. It was not for another two years that the awarding of government air mail contracts to private airlines made commercial aviation feasible, and then only for carrying freight. When that happened, Dickinson was ready.

He outbid the well-financed National Air Transport on a government contract for air mail service between Chicago and St. Paul after being told by NAT officials in a prebid conference that he would never get the contract. When NAT then tried to prevent him from obtaining engines for his plane, he borrowed three from an old friend, William A. Moffet, former commander of Great Lakes Naval Training Center, and with characteristic vigor set out to get his new airline off the ground. Unfortunately, the new airline was not only undercapitalized, but Dickinson, in his anger at NAT, submitted a bid too low to enable him to recover costs.

However, he hired some of the nation's finest pilots and proceeded to launch his airline. The pilots included Elmer Partridge, his old friend; Nimo Black; Alfred O. Sporrer; David Behncke, who later founded the Air Line Pilots Association; Emil (Matty) Laird; Henry (Pop) Keller; William Brock; and possibly the best pilot of that time, Ervin E. Ballough. With the motto of his new airline painted on the sides of his Laird Speedwing planes—"Celerity-Certainty-Security"—

94

E. L. Partridge and His Training Plane

Elmer Partridge in front of one of his trainers at Ashburn in 1925. (ALFRED O. SPORRER COLLECTION)

95

Dickinson spent his last years collecting tickets for inaugural runs on
new air routes and attending air races. He is shown in Miami in 1932
with Alfred O. Sporrer (left) and E. M. (Matty) Laird (right). (ALFRED
O. SPORRER COLLECTION)

Dickinson was ready to inaugurate service on June 6, 1926.

It was a disaster. The day was windy and a dust storm from the southwest made visibility poor. Partridge, who had flown to Minneapolis the day before in his plane specially modified with a new 200-horsepower engine, was killed in a crash a few minutes after taking off for Chicago. He and Dickinson had been close friends for years, and the old man cried when he heard the news. Meanwhile, Laird, Keller, and Black had been forced down at LaCrosse, Wisconsin, because of the storm, and only Black was able to continue on to Minneapolis.

The new airline was never able to recover from that disastrous start. On June 21, Dickinson's pilots went on strike, contending that he had failed to provide them with fast or safe planes. Dickinson claimed that the amount of mail being carried was insufficient to support the service. One pilot, Dan Kaiser, of Milwaukee, said that Dickinson had only one plane that met safety standards.[10] The airline was nearly shut down for a week in August when Ballough was the only pilot willing to continue flying, and Dickinson contemplated cutting back service from seven days a week to five because there wasn't enough mail to justify the service. Finally on August 17, after Ballough was forced down near LaCrosse, Dickinson called it quits and notified the Post Office Department that he was giving them the required forty-five days' notice before halting service.[11]

He then shrugged off his third failure at starting an airline and turned his attention to airplane racing—a rage that was sweeping the country at the time. Dickinson bought two powerful Laird Commercials which Ballough flew for him. Dickinson considered Ballough his personal pilot and flew in almost every race with him. In 1927 they finished second in a cross country race between New York and Spokane, Washington, which was won by Dickinson's friend and sometime racing partner Charles (Speed) Holman. The next year Dickinson and Ballough finished second in the National Air Races in Los Angeles, and in January, 1929, they set a new record time of nine hours and fifty-nine minutes between Miami and Chicago. The team was broken up May 17, 1931, when Holman was killed in an air show in Omaha.

Dickinson finally obtained a government pilot's license in September 21, 1930, at age 72, although he had made a solo flight at the controls as early as February 13, 1921, after taking flying lessons from Partridge at Ashburn Field.

In his final years, Dickinson spent much of his time on an unusual hobby with Father James Organisciak, a Catholic priest. They collected tickets on inaugural flights on the then rapidly expanding airline industry. Before he died, he had collected thirteen airline tickets bearing the number one, which indicated an inaugural flight.

On September 2, 1935, Dickinson was stricken with a fatal heart attack while in New York to see a doctor treating his heart disease. Seven days later, his friends Al Sporrer and Ballough emptied an urn containing his ashes from George Horton's airplane five hundred feet over Lake Michigan near Grant Park, as had been his request.

1. They were found after his death in the North Clark Street warehouse in which he had placed them and sold for $3,000 at a probate court auction, according to the June 30, 1936, *Chicago Tribune*.

2. On Sept. 7, 1912, Dickinson lost the $500 weekly payroll for the men working on the *America Defender* after withdrawing the money from his account in the Northern Trust Bank. After discovering the loss, he withdrew another $500.

3. *Chicago Tribune*, Sept. 8, 1912.

4. *Chicago Tribune*, Oct. 1, 1929.

5. Ye Ham, a Chinese pilot, was hired to maintain the bunkhouse and cook for the pilots.

6. Dickinson had been instrumental in 1922 in convincing the Cook County Forest Preserve District to develop Checkerboard Field as a publicly-owned airport after a disastrous fire that wiped out most of the privately owned facilities there.

7. As late as 1932 Dickinson was still involved in Ashburn Field. On June 14 of that year he was charged with operating an airport without a license, in violation of state law.

8. An indication of how seriously underpowered the Lawson transport was can be obtained from comparing it with two successful commercial transports from the next decade, the Boeing-247 and Douglas DC-3. The Lawson plane had two 400-horsepower engines to move a 14,000-pound airplane (gross weight). The B-247, which was also considered underpowered, had two 550-horsepower engines and a gross weight of 13,650 pounds. Later model DC-3s used two 1,200-horsepower engines to pull a gross weight of 28,000 pounds.

9. *Chicago Tribune*, Dec. 30, 1923.

10. Despite the contentions of some of his pilots, Dickinson had some concern for aviation safety. Shortly before he closed his airline, he was approached for a job by an unemployed young pilot named Charles Lindbergh, who had a reputation for parachuting from his mail planes in bad weather rather than attempting to land them safely. Dickinson curtly refused to hire Lindbergh, who went on to fame by making the first solo flight across the Atlantic Ocean.

11. The Post Office Department then awarded the contract to the newly formed, Detroit-based Northwest Airways, which evolved into Northwest Orient Airlines.

Even experienced pilots had trouble with Ashburn Field's cinder runway. Capt. Roy Brown piled up this plane on the runway in 1917.
(C. R. SINCLAIR COLLECTION)

The World War

When World War I finally became impossible for the United States to ignore, the nation was characteristically unprepared and without an air force worthy of the name, despite warnings from the aviation community dating back more than a decade. The air forces of the European powers were somewhat better prepared for the war that erupted on July 28, 1914, when Austria declared war on Serbia, than was the United States nearly thirty-three months later, when it entered the conflict. If the European powers can be excused for their failure to recognize fully the potential of the flying machine in war, the United States cannot; by the time it declared war on April 6, 1917, aviation had become an integral part of the war in Europe.

Understandably, the early aviation pioneers recognized the military potential of the airplane long before the War Department came to a similar conclusion. The Wright brothers, at the urging of Octave Chanute, tried to interest the War Department in their flying machine soon after they developed it. In October, 1905, the War Department's Board of Ordnance and Fortification wrote to the Wrights telling them that their invention had no military use, which prompted Chanute to remark: "Those fellows are a bunch of asses."

When the 1911 international air show was held in Chicago, one of the events was a bombing contest in which aviators tried to hit a battleship-shaped target on the ground with sacks of flour. The next year the Aero Club of Illinois actively lobbied President William Howard Taft to sign a military aviation bill establishing, among other things, an aerial reconnaissance unit.[1] Just before the outbreak of the war in Europe in 1914, the Aero Club actively campaigned to have the Navy open a seaplane base in Chicago. At the time, many Aero Club members had followed the lead of McCormick and become interested in hydroplanes.

Later that month came the first positive indication in years that Washington had noticed the war clouds gathering over Europe. Lee Hammond, secretary of the Aero Club, was asked on April 24 to serve as chairman of a technical committee to determine what the government would require of civil aviation in the United States should war occur. Hammond completed an inventory of civil aircraft in the Chicago area and forwarded it to Washington in just six days with the notation: "Some of them (airplanes), as stated in the report, are not much for looks, but I would respectfully recall the fact that the machine with which Glenn Curtiss won the Gordon Bennett Cup was ridiculed by foreign aviators and described as a 'pile of junk.' Yet it brought home the bacon."[2]

Chicago was far removed from the battlefields of Europe when war broke out in the summer of 1914, and there was little that Chicago aviators could do but continue to lobby for increased American preparedness. A few pilots decided to go to Europe and offer their services to Great Britain or France. Probably the best known of that group was Norman Prince, a member of a prominent Boston family who had been sent to Chicago to practice law and had become involved in Aero Club activities. Soon after the war began, Prince and his brother, Frederick, volunteered their services as aviators to the French. Norman Prince was one of the organizers of the famous Escadrille Americaine, later known as Lafayette Escadrille.

The Prince brothers had been polo enthusiasts before the war, but Norman decided to take up aviation against the wishes of his father, Frederick H. Prince, chairman of the executive board of Armour & Company. Under an assumed name, George Mannor, he went from

Boston to Atlanta to obtain a pilot's license. His father promptly shipped him to a Chicago law firm in 1912, but he quickly became involved in Aero Club activities and later that year submitted the winning design for the *America Defender*.

In the war, Prince flew with such skill that he became the first ace from the Chicago area, shooting down the five German planes needed to win the designation. He was shot down once. Probably his best known escapade occurred in August, 1916, when he inadvertently landed next to a German trench and was captured. Two German officers forced him at pistol point to take them on a reconnaissance flight over French lines. He escaped when he noticed that neither German had fastened his seat belt and promptly looped the loop, causing his passengers to fall to their deaths.

Two months later, on October 6, he barely escaped death in a dogfight when a German pilot shot away part of a wing and some of the supporting wires on his airplane. Prince nursed the plane back to friendly lines, however.

The French were sufficiently impressed with his combat record to promote him from sergeant to lieutenant and award him the Legion of Honor. Soon thereafter, he was detailed with his squadron to protect a French night flight of bombers in a raid against an arms factory in Oberndorf, Germany. He survived a dogfight against German planes attempting to defend the factory, but later suffered a head wound from anti-aircraft fire from the ground. Prince got his plane back to the French airdrome, but crashed while attempting to land and broke both legs. He died a week later (October 15, 1916) of the head injury in a hospital in Alsace—the third American aviator killed in the war.[3]

In Chicago, Aero Club members continued their marginally successful campaign to upgrade military aviation in the United States. Dickinson had published an article in *Flying Magazine* suggesting that the sinking of the steamship *Lusitania* by a German submarine May 7, 1915, could have been avoided with adequate aerial reconnaissance.[4]

The next month, many Aero Club members joined the National Airplane Fund to raise money for military aviation. The fund's organizers lamented that at the time (July, 1915) the United States had fewer than twenty aircraft available to the Army and Navy. Jay J.

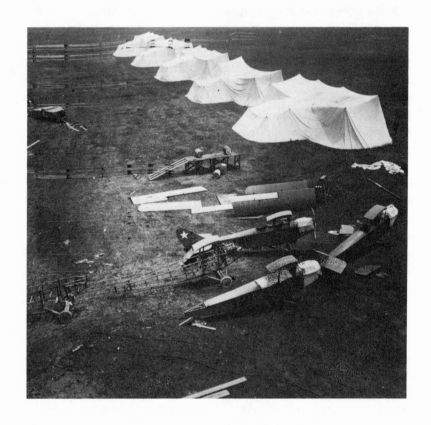

War came to Chicago in October, 1916, months before Congress declared it, when the Army Signal Corps set up hangar tents and began assembling planes for a pilot training school to be established at Ashburn Field. (CHICAGO HISTORICAL SOCIETY)

McCarthy, Aero Club publicity chairman, publicly criticized Congressman James R. Mann, of Chicago, for opposing the appropriation in Congress for Navy hydroplanes.

The United States was not much better prepared two years later when war was declared. A few months after Congress acted, the nation agreed to a French request to build and equip an air force with 4,500 planes, 5,000 pilots, and 50,000 mechanics. At the time, America owned only about 100 military airplanes, and it was estimated that there were no more than 1,000 skilled aviators— civilian and military—in the country.

By 1916, the War Department had become aware that an air force would be necessary if the nation entered World War I. On June 28 of that year the Aero Club of Illinois offered the War Department the free use of Ashburn Field as a training base for military pilots,[5] and the government accepted the invitation three months later and announced that a Signal Corps detachment would be sent there. Club members promptly met and agreed to undertake a fund-raising campaign to pay for the buildings the military facility would need. The club also held a public flying exhibition at Ashburn October 28 to celebrate the arrival of the military detachment that day.

John T. McCutcheon, the cartoonist and aviation promoter, had enlisted in the Army Air Service a few days before and took his first flying lesson in a military biplane while a crowd of 500, some of whom had taken a Wabash Railroad train from the Loop, watched. The installation was relatively primitive: the four Army aircraft used tents for hangars, and the five Signal Corps aviators, commanded by Capt. Joseph C. Morrow, lived in tents. Military pilots were so scarce that the installation's three principal flight instructors were civilians— Theodore MacCaulay, A. Livingstone Allen, and J.D. Hill. Allen was the only veteran of aerial combat in the group. Early in 1916 he had enlisted in the British Royal Flying Corps and spent three weeks directing artillery fire from an airplane. He returned to the United States that year to teach flying.

The Ashburn military installation was short lived, however, because of the difficulty of attempting to train pilots during the cold Chicago winter. In early February, 1917, the Army packed its equipment onto a train and moved it to Memphis. The Aero Club simply geared up a campaign to have it replaced, and on April 16, ten days after the United States declared war on Germany, the War Department decided that it would have to have an installation in Chicago after all. The government planned to ship as many as 48 Curtiss airplanes to Chicago to train up to 75 pilots, and the Aero Club lobbied to have Ashburn Field designated as the site of the facility.

The War Department was at first agreeable, and attempted to buy additional land adjacent to Ashburn before discovering that the price was too high. That led to the decision to buy cheaper farm land somewhere outside the Chicago area. Because the University of Illinois at Champaign-Urbana in May had been designated as one of six ground schools to give flight preparatory training to potential pilots, the Signal Corps later that month picked a square mile of farm land in Rantoul, just north of Champaign and about 110 miles south of Chicago, as the site of the new base. The War Department concurred in the selection May 21 and construction began the next day. The newly established 4th Aviation School Squadron began its work at Ashburn Field while construction continued in Rantoul.

The transfer of the squadron to Rantoul on July 16 was something of an air show in itself—the largest movement of men and material by air attempted in the United States.[6] Lieutenant W. W. Spain and E. A. Johnson, a civilian instructor, flew to Rantoul from Ashburn July 3 to plot the course the air fleet would later take. Before the official opening of newly named Chanute Field July 16, twenty-two military planes, each carrying a passenger, took off at one-minute intervals from Ashburn and flew there. The pilot of the twenty-third plane, Fred A. Hoover, got lost and finally landed in St. Joseph, Michigan.

Before the war ended in late 1918, thousands of military aviators had been trained at Chanute, many of them from among the 2,644 graduates of the University of Illinois military aviation school as well as the reserve officer training programs. The system produced a number of successful combat pilots, including several aces with five or more enemy aircraft shot down to their credit. One, Reed G. Landis, who later commanded aviation units in World War II and the Korean War, was the nation's sixth leading American ace of the war with 12

Lieutenant R. W. (Shorty) Schroeder, who set a new world altitude record of 33,000 feet on Feb. 27, 1920. (C.R. SINCLAIR COLLECTION)

Chicago World War I ace Reed Landis always flew an airplane numbered 13. He also insisted on staying on the 13th floor of hotels in a room numbered 13. (KEENE LANDIS COLLECTION)

enemy aircraft shot down. Other Chicago aces included William P. Erwin, with nine aircraft; Frank K. Hays, six; and John J. Seerley, Duerson (Dewey) Knight, Lawrence K. Callahan, and Victor Strahm, each with five.[7]

Landis, the son of Kennesaw Mountain Landis, the commissioner of professional baseball and a federal judge, left home at age 19 to enlist in the First Illinois Cavalry and serve on the Mexican border. The following year the United States entered World War I, and Landis was accepted in the officers' training program at Fort Sheridan, north of Chicago. From there he volunteered for the training programs at Champaign and Rantoul.

He was sent overseas in August, 1917, for assignment to the British air service for additional training and went to the front in March, 1918, with the 40th Squadron of the Royal Flying Corps. On his first day in actual combat the next month, he downed a German plane in a frontal shootout. Landis' plane was heavily damaged, but he got it back to his base.[8]

His finest day of the war occurred August 8. While on patrol in the Douai sector, he became involved in a dogfight, shooting down two enemy planes and a balloon in just twelve minutes. He caught both planes by surprise and shot them down before they could return fire, then leisurely downed the reconnaissance balloon they were supposed to be protecting.

Later he nearly lost his life after successfully attacking a German reconnaissance plane. While pursuing the damaged plane downward to apply the coup de grace, two ammunition drums in Landis' plane rolled forward and jammed the rear rudder pedal bar. His plane plunged uncontrollably until he was able to knock the drums loose, using his signal pistol as a hammer, and pull out of the dive just two hundred feet above the ground.

From March through September 15, 1918, when he was reassigned from the British forces to command of the newly formed U.S. 25th Aero Squadron, he shot down five enemy planes and a balloon. He was later awarded the British Distinguished Flying Cross and American Distinguished Service Cross, albeit somewhat belatedly in 1934, because his service records had been lost.

Landis, by then a major, returned to Chicago February 7, 1919, on the Twentieth Century Limited and somewhat bashfully told reporters: "Really there is no story to tell. I just got them and that's all."[9] After the war he decided against a career in flying and went into the advertising business, although he continued to maintain an interest in aviation. He testified for the defense in the 1925 trial by court martial of General William (Billy) Mitchell, the nation's chief prophet of air power, and four years later was appointed to a special Cook County coroner's jury investigating the deaths of four persons in a mid-air collision over suburban Northbrook.

He strongly criticized the practice common at the time of allowing the county sheriff, whose staff rarely had anyone with much aviation experience, to enforce federal and local air safety standards. On March 3, 1929, he wrote to Illinois Governor Louis T. Emmerson urging the state to enforce air safety regulations strictly, despite a reluctance on the part of the state because it might impede the development of that industry. "With the enormous growth of aviation during the last year, however, it becomes necessary to have a set of ironclad rules governing the conduct of the industry," Landis wrote.[10]

Emmerson soon appointed him as a member of the newly formed Illinois Aerial Navigation Commission and, on August 31, 1931, as chairman of the Illinois Aeronautics Commission, an agency set up to regulate pilots and airports.

In 1940, Landis was appointed regional vice president in Chicago for American Airways, a post he held for only a year before taking a leave of absence to accept an appointment by New York Mayor Fiorello LaGuardia to organize the civil defense program—an organization being formed in anticipation of World War II. In that war he was commander of the Army Air Corps troop carrier unit[11] and in the Korean War he commanded the 437th Reserve Troop Carrier Wing. By then a colonel, Landis was that unit's commander at O'Hare Field until his retirement from the Air Force in 1953. He died May 30, 1975, at age 78, in a lodge he owned near Hot Springs, Arkansas.

The Army was not the only branch of the service to open a base in the Chicago area in World War I. The same month that Chanute Field opened (July, 1917) an unusual air squadron was formed at the Great Lakes Naval Training Center north of Chicago, primarily through the efforts of Lee Hammond, Aero Club secretary, and Dickinson, who

110

talked Captain William A. Moffet, Great Lakes commander, into the idea. The new unit was given the nickname "The Navy's Millionaire Squadron" because many of its members came from wealthy Chicago-area families, including Philip K. Wrigley, William Mitchell, Ellsworth Buck, Emery Wilder, Alfred Wolff, William McCormick Blair, Albert Dewey, Allister McCormick, and Logan A. (Jack) Vilas, the early hydroplane enthusiast.[1][2] Hammond was commissioned a lieutenant and was in charge of the training on the unit's three seaplanes.

The unit was short lived, however. It was disbanded in October, 1917, just a few months after being formed, when several officials in Washington objected to the unit. Moffet later became a rear admiral in charge of the Navy's Bureau of Aeronautics.

1. James S. Stephens, Aero Club vice president and general manager, in a letter of July 2, 1912, to President Taft in Aero Club files.

2. Hammond letter of July 2, 1912, in Aero Club files.

3. Frederick H. Prince finally managed to have his son's body returned to the United States for burial in Washington in 1937.

4. *Flying Magazine*, June, 1915.

5. Telegram of June 28, 1916, from Aero Club in Aero Club files.

6. Scott Field near Belleville, a St. Louis suburb, became the second Army aviation training facility in Illinois when it opened Aug. 12, 1917.

7. Differing methods of counting credit for enemy aircraft shot down have resulted in conflicting totals for many aviators in World War I. The confusion is compounded because many American aviators served part of their war tour with British, French, or Italian units. The British system gave Landis twelve "kills", but he is credited with only ten by the American system. Other pilots had similar differences in scores. The following is a list of Chicago-area pilots credited with kills by the American system as recorded in *U.S. Air Service Victory Credit*, USAF Historical Study-N. 133, Historical Research Division, Aerospace Studies Institute, Air University, Maxwell Air Force Base, Ala., June, 1969.

The Combat Records of Chicago-area aviators in World War I:

Pilot—Unit	Credits
Charles P. Anderson—96th BMR	1*
William J. Armstrong—17th PUR	1
John M. Baker—20th BMR	1*
Herbert B. Bartholf—103rd PUR	2*
Charles R. Blake	1*

Raymond C. Bridgman—139th PUR   4*
Thomas P. Butz—95th PUR   1*
Lawrence K. Callahan—148th PUR   2
Everett R. Cook—91st OBS   5*
Edward K. Delana—91st OBS   1*
Raymond P. Dillon—24th OBS   4*
Charles R. Dolive—93rd PUR   1*
Robert W. Donaldson—27th PUR   1*
George C. Dorsey—148th PUR   2
William P. Erwin—1st OBS   8*
Farnum Fish   1
Roswell H. Fuller   2*
Percy W. Graham—49th PUR   1*
Andre H. Gundelach—96thBMR   2*
John R. Harrington—13th PUR   6*
Frank K. Hays—13th PUR   6*
Eugene B. Jones—103rd PUR   2*
Duerson Knight   1
Reed G. Landis   10
Edward K. MacDonald   1*
Richard P. Mathews—20th BMR   1*
Linn D. Merrill—166th BMR   2*
Paul D. Nelson—11th BMR   3*
Russel H. Pedler—166th BMR   2*
Josiah J. Pegues—95th PUR   2*
Henry J. Popperfuss—95th PUR   1
Harold H. Sayre—11th BMR   1*
Harry A. Sclotzhauer   1*
George V. Sejbold—148th PUR   3
William H. Shearman—17th PUR   1
Walter A. Stahl—11th BMR   1*
William H. Vail—95th PUR   1*
John Wentworth—49th PUR   1*
Alan F. Winslow—94th PUR   2*

* Indicates a credit shared with other aviators.

8. *Chicago Herald and Examiner*, Jan. 29, 1928.

9. *Chicago Tribune*, Feb. 8, 1919.

10. Landis letter of Mar. 30, 1929, to Gov. Emmerson.

11. Landis' son, Keehn, flew a P-51 Mustang in combat in World War II and was credited with shooting down one enemy plane.

12. Alfred Wolff, last surviving member of the Unit, in a February, 1979, interview.

The First Disaster

Although airplanes were a rarity in Chicago's skies in 1917 and 1918 because of wartime restrictions on civil aviation, residents of the South Side often saw another type of airship. B.F. Goodrich and Goodyear Tire and Rubber companies used a hangar at White City Amusement Park, 63rd Street and South Park Avenue, to complete the assembly of Navy blimps. The White City hangar apparently had been used for balloon exhibitions before World War I and was the closest available building to Akron large enough to handle blimps in May, 1917, when the companies were commissioned to build some for the Navy. Construction on Goodyear's new airship hangar at Wingfoot Lake, near Akron, had not been completed, so the company built the parts for blimps in Akron and shipped them to Chicago for final assembly at White City.[1]

The first Goodyear blimp built in Chicago for Navy coastal patrols was the B-1. The White City hangar was not quite large enough to accommodate the completed airship, so a trench was dug along the centerline of the building to permit the observation cars to be attached below the gas bag, or envelope, as it is sometimes called. The crew sent from Akron completed work on the B-1 and on May 29, 1917, it began its flight to Akron to be turned over to the Navy. Ralph H. Upson, winner of the 1913 international balloon race and James Gordon Bennett Cup in Paris that year, was at the controls of the 160-foot airship as it rose above White City one midnight and headed into the darkness over Lake Michigan.

Sometime later, Goodyear completed its Wingfoot Lake hangar and transferred all its airship operations there, although Goodrich took over the White City facility temporarily and built as many as five Navy B-ships there from September, 1917, through June, 1918, before moving back to Akron.[2]

Thus in 1919, when Goodyear began looking for a building in which to assemble the company's first commercial blimp, White City was the obvious choice. The Navy was still using the Wingfoot Lake base, and it was not available to the company for commercial operations. Like the Navy's B ships before it, the components of the new blimp were built in Akron and shipped to Chicago for final assembly. The new airship had evolved from the Navy's B types with two major improvements: the envelope was segmented into compartments, or ballonets, to prevent it from crashing should a rupture occur; and the propellers were mounted in front of the two Gnome engines instead of in the rear, as was usual.

The new blimp, like its predecessors, had an open gondola. Its gas bag was filled with 95,000 cubic feet of volatile hydrogen, the standard element then used to inflate airships. The safer helium, which had first been identified spectroscopically in 1868 but had not been isolated until 1895, was still too expensive in 1919 to use in blimps; it cost $125 per thousand cubic feet, compared with $5 for hydrogen.

The parts for the airship were completed in Akron and shipped to Chicago June 29, 1919. Final assembly on the $100,000 vehicle was completed at White City in July, and by July 21 it was ready for its maiden flight. It was named *Wingfoot Air Express* for Goodyear's Akron-to-Boston trucking subsidiary, which began operations in 1916.[3] The name Wingfoot refers to the Goodyear corporate logotype.

At 9 a.m., Goodyear pilot John A. Boettner climbed into the ten-passenger car with mechanics Henry Wacker and Carl (Buck) Weaver and Army Colonel Joseph C. Morrow, an observer, and started the

The Goodyear blimp *Wingfoot* at Grant Park before its crash. The
Chicago Yacht Club is in the background. (GOODYEAR AEROSPACE
CORPORATION)

One of the engines of the *Wingfoot* is seen amid the charred wreckage
of the lobby of the Illinois Trust and Savings Bank. (CHICAGO
TRIBUNE)

engines. The *Wingfoot* rose gracefully and headed north for Grant Park. Boettner and Morrow testified later that the flight was uneventful, and the airship was moored in Grant Park for a while to allow the crowd gathered there to look it over. Just before noon, Boettner took off for a trip north along the lake shore to Diversey Avenue, returning to Grant Park at about 3 p.m. without a hint of trouble.

About an hour later, Boettner was ready to return to White City. He took along as passengers, in addition to his two mechanics, Earl Davenport, the publicist for White City, and William G. Norton, a photographer for the *Chicago Herald and Examiner*. Norton apparently wanted to take some aerial photographs of the Loop, so Boettner flew west over the downtown area instead of south along the lake shore.

Boettner said later that he was flying at approximately forty to forty-five miles an hour at 1,200 feet when he felt heat from a fire. "Looking back (at the tail), I saw shots of fire on both sides of the rear of the bag. I watched the flames for a couple of seconds before I said anything to the other fellows. Knowing the ship was finished, I yelled, 'Over the top, everybody.' As I yelled I felt the frame [buckle], but by this time they were beginning to slide over the sides," he testified later.

Within seconds, the *Wingfoot* was a flaming holocaust plunging downward toward a building on the northwest corner of La Salle Street and Jackson Boulevard, occupied by Illinois Trust and Savings Bank. The bank had closed for business for the day, but scores of employees were still inside completing their accounting of the day's transactions. The flaming *Wingfoot* crashed through the skylight on the roof of the building and onto the main business floor, the gasoline from its fuel tanks exploding upon impact.

Thirteen people died in the disaster—ten bank employees who burned to death in the fire or were crushed by falling debris and three of the airship passengers. Twenty-eight bank employees were injured. It was the first disaster in the history of civil aviation. Boettner[4] parachuted safely onto the roof of a nearby building, as did Wacker. However, Weaver was killed after his parachute caught fire from the blimp and he fell through the skylight and into the fire below. Norton was fatally injured when he lost control of his parachute and crashed

117

into a nearby building. He died the next day, asking, according to newspaper legend, whether the photographs he made had been saved. Davenport, the only person to ride the car down, died when he was impaled on the bank roof.

Even before the fire had been extinguished, Cook County law enforcement officials had begun an investigation of the incident. Boettner was arrested on the scene, and State's Attorney Maclay Hoyne ordered the arrest of sixteen other Goodyear employees for possible criminal prosecution. Coroner Peter Hoffman impaneled a special jury and took them to the scene. At an emergency meeting that night, just six hours after the crash, the City Council drew up a resolution instructing the corporation counsel to draft an ordinance that would give the city control of airships and airplanes flying over its corporate limits. The resolution had been introduced by Anton Cermak, an influential and ambitious alderman, who urged an outright ban on flying over Chicago: "This accident shows we must stop flying over the city sooner or later, and we better do it sooner."

Boettner and the other Goodyear employees taken into custody were never brought to trial because there was no evidence to indicate that a crime had been committed. William C. Young, head of Goodyear's aeronautics department, later gave the opinion that static electricity in the air or, more probably, hot oil that spewed onto the gas-filled envelope was the probable cause of the fire. Boettner at first suggested static electricity, but later theorized that sparks from the engine blown back against the envelope were the cause.[5] However, the cause was never officially determined.

Probably the most immediate result of the *Wingfoot* disaster, the political furor notwithstanding, was the decision by Goodyear to use nonflammable helium for inflating its airships. Improvements in the process used to isolate helium and increased demand for it from the military and Goodyear resulted in a decrease in its price to less than $20 per thousand cubic feet. That was still four times the price of hydrogen but, in the opinion of the nation's airship community, the added cost was justifiable because of the increase in safety.[6]

Safety was also, of course, the subject of the public debate that ensued after the crash, although the most important aspect of that debate concerned whether aviation needed to be regulated and by whom. A few days after the accident, Reed G. Landis, by virtue of his war record one of the city's more respected aviators, suggested to the Aero Club of Illinois that a committee be appointed to "investigate the necessity for aerial regulations and laws and that this committee offer co-operation to the governor of the State of Illinois and to whatever municipal committee had been appointed by [Chicago Mayor William Hale] Thompson for consideration of the situation." Landis also recommended that aircraft that had not passed a safety inspection be prohibited from flying over Chicago and that no plane be allowed to fly over a populated area at so low an altitude that it could not glide to an open field in the event of engine failure.[7]

The prime concern of Aero Club of Illinois members was which government would regulate aviation; they favored federal, not local, controls. Friendly Aldermen George W. Maypole and Dorsey Crowe, members of the City Aviation Commission, were persuaded that federal regulation would be better and when they traveled to New York City were given a letter of introduction to Aero Club of America officers to help reinforce the local club's position. "We have tried to impress upon this commission the advisability of working for national control, approved by state legislation, and the advisability of avoiding any local legislation, depending rather upon the control of those in charge of flying fields," James S. Stephens of the Illinois club wrote to his colleagues in New York.[8]

There was a brief flurry of activity on Capitol Hill in Washington after the disaster, including several congressional hearings and a few impassioned speeches. However, the nation was not ready for aviation regulation, and Congress turned its attention to the more pressing problems of a nation trying to adjust from war to peace. The furor in Chicago also subsided under the crush of post-war problems and the strong anti-regulation lobby of the Aero Club. Front page stories about the *Wingfoot* quickly yielded to stories about a bitter streetcar strike, race riots, a sensational child murder case, a revolution in Mexico, and the Chicago White Sox winning the American League pennant. In the end, the City Council adopted a watered-down version of the Cermak ordinance that banned flying over the Loop and heavily populated areas of Chicago except with a permit from the commissioner of public works, who was also empowered to establish

119

regulations governing such flights.[9]

Despite the failure of Congress to pass any regulatory statutes pertaining to aviation after the *Wingfoot* disaster, the pressure for such regulation continued until another disaster forced the enactment of the Air Commerce Act of 1926. As early as 1916, the Aero Club of America had put forth a proposal to create a separate aeronautical department under the secretary of war. That, in effect, happened in World War I when President Woodrow Wilson issued a proclamation restricting flying over the United States except with a license from the War Department. However, the restriction was for security reasons, not safety, and it expired in July, 1919, just before the fatal *Wingfoot* flight.

By 1918, the National Advisory Commission for Aeronautics (NACA) had concluded that "federal legislation should be enacted governing the navigation of aircraft in the United States." NACA's executive committee ultimately drafted a bill creating such a regulatory agency under the jurisdiction of the Department of Commerce, and Wilson in February, 1919, endorsed it. Several bills based on that proposal were finally introduced in Congress in 1920, but the issue became lost in the dispute over suggestions by the controversial Army Air Service brigadier general, Billy Mitchell, that a separate cabinet-level Aviation Department be created with jurisdiction over civil and military aviation.

Meanwhile, a young former World War I aviator and Chicago attorney, William P. MacCracken, Jr., had become interested in the subject of aviation law, or what there was of it in those days, and through his work on various American Bar Association committees in the early 1920s induced that group to recommend federal regulation of aviation. In the 1920s MacCracken was probably the most significant figure in the nation in establishing a federal regulatory system for aviation.

Although the nation's political bodies usually respond with safety legislation only after a disaster, many congressmen had become concerned with the high post-war toll of human life in barnstorming exhibitions. Typical was the case of 18-year-old daredevil Louis James, who was killed July 3, 1922, while attempting to climb between airplanes in an exhibition over Ashburn Field. He had just grabbed a

Typical of the post-war barnstormers was Lillian Boyer, shown
hanging from the wing of a plane above Hawthorne Race Track in
Cicero in the early 1920s. The tongue-in-cheek note at the bottom was
to C. R. Sinclair. (C. R. SINCLAIR COLLECTION)

rope ladder suspended from one plane when the aircraft he had left swerved into him and he was cut to pieces by the propeller.

Congress continued to debate the various regulatory proposals without accomplishing much of anything and was seemingly oblivious to the type of accident that killed James until, in early 1925, the Air Mail Act was passed. It gave the Post Office Department's Air Mail Service to private contractors. It was by then obvious to a majority of Congress that some sort of regulation was needed, if for no other reason than to protect the mail. However, nothing was accomplished until later that year, when there occurred within a week of each other two "disasters" that finally drove home to Capitol Hill the necessity for regulation. On August 31, a Navy seaplane with a crew of five disappeared on a flight to Hawaii, and on September 3 the giant Navy dirigible *Shenandoah* broke up during a storm over Ava, Ohio, and fourteen of her crew of forty-five died in the ensuing crash.

The houses of Congress quickly passed somewhat differing aviation bills requiring for the first time the licensing of pilots and federal registration of aircraft. The Senate version required such regulation only in the case of interstate commerce, and it was that version that ultimately emerged from the conference committee and was signed by President Calvin Coolidge May 20, 1926.

The law gave to the Department of Commerce the power to administer the new act, and Secretary of Commerce Herbert Hoover asked Chicagoan Paul Henderson, who had resigned as head of the Air Mail Service to help organize the new National Air Transport, to accept the appointment as assistant secretary of commerce for aviation. Henderson declined, but Rep. Martin Madden—a Chicagoan and Henderson's father-in-law—insisted that the job go to a resident of his home town. MacCracken was offered the post, accepted, and was instrumental in drafting the federal air regulations.[10]

1. James L. Shock, *American Airship Bases and Facilities,* manuscript planned for publication, Airship International Press, Bloomington, Ill., 1979.

2. The building used as a hangar was converted into a roller rink after the war. It was destroyed by fire in 1925.

3. Zenon Hansen, *The Goodyear Airships*, Airship International Press, Bloomington, Ill., 1977, p. 1.

4. Boettner, who went on to log more than 10,000 hours in airships, died March 17, 1961, at age 68.

5. *Chicago Tribune*, July 22, 23, 24, 1919.

6. Hansen, p. 1.

7. Landis letter of Aug. 1, 1919, in Aero Club files.

8. Stephens letter of Aug. 1, 1919, to Aero Club of America, in Aero Club files.

9. City Council ordinance, December, 1919.

10. Nick A Komons, *Bonfires to Beacons: Federal Aviation Policy under the Air Commerce Act 1916-38*, U.S. Department of Transportation, 1978, pp. 87-88.

Ben Lipsner (center with moustache) stands between air mail pilots Ed
Gardner (left) and Max Miller during a war exposition in Chicago in
September, 1918, following their flights inaugurating air mail service
between New York and Chicago. Charles Dickinson (far left) and
Augustus Post (far right) of the Aero Club of America, also posed.
(CHICAGO HISTORICAL SOCIETY)

The Air Mail

Benjamin B. Lipsner was probably the first of a new breed of men in aviation—an enterprise that until he came along was almost solely the province of adventurers, daredevils, entrepreneurs, inventors, and men rich enough to afford such expensive toys as airplanes. Lipsner was neither a pilot nor a tinkerer; his sole interest in aviation was that it was potentially a new mode of transportation that could be used, like trucks, to carry the commerce of the nation. He was a professional manager, and he applied his skills and the federal government's wealth toward making a success of aviation's first sustained commercial venture—the air mail.

On September 4, 1918, Lipsner returned to his home town of Chicago for a quick inspection of Grant Park, the field he had selected for the U.S. Post Office Department's first test air mail flight between Chicago and New York City the next day. He had been on hand the previous May 15 with President Wilson at Washington's Polo Grounds to watch the inauguration of the air mail service between there and Philadelphia and New York. However, the New York to Chicago route was considered far riskier because of the longer distance involved and the necessity for flying over the Allegheny

Mountains. In those days, flying over the Allegheny Mountains was considered dangerous because of unusual air currents, downdrafts, and bad weather.

For months Lipsner had planned the route of the experimental path-finding flights from Belmont Park in New York with refueling stops in Lock Haven, Pennsylvania; Cleveland; and Bryan, Ohio, to Chicago's Grant Park. He had also hand picked the two pilots, Max Miller and Edward V. Gardner. To justify the proposed service to the Post Office, Lipsner had computed that the mail could be carried by plane between those two cities in about nine and a half hours, compared with the more than twenty-four hours necessary by train.

Early September 5, Lipsner stationed himself beside a telephone in the main Chicago Post Office to await a telephone call from Belmont Park telling him everything was ready to start. "Come on, let's go," he impatiently told the starter when the call finally came, and a few minutes later at 7:08 a.m. (New York time) Miller took off. Although the flights were scheduled to take twelve hours, Lipsner anxiously waited for the better part of two days for the pilots to call him when they made their scheduled stops. Both had difficulty with the weather over Pennsylvania and Gardner was plagued with mechanical difficulties. Miller finally reached Chicago at 6:55 p.m. September 6. Gardner, who had been forced down by darkness in Westville, Indiana, arrived the next day.[1] Together, they carried about four hundred pounds of mail.

Although the two flights took considerably longer than the railway postal service, Lipsner was convinced that, with proper organization, the service would be successful. When scheduled service began in May, 1919, it used planes and trains for awhile. The airplanes carried the mail on the first segment of the route in daylight and trains made the remainder of the run at night. It was hardly a satisfactory arrangement, even by the standards of that day, but it did allow the air mail service to continue until the development of better aircraft permitted non-stop flights between Chicago and New York.

For Lipsner, the air mail represented a somewhat surprising change in career, although he had a brush with aviation as early as 1910, when he read in a Chicago newspaper about flying activities at Clearing Field, 65th Street and Major Avenue, and went to see what

The Douglas World Cruiser *Chicago* on display at Maywood Field in 1924 before being one of the two planes to successfully complete a 26,345-mile around-the-world flight. The plane is now on display in the National Air and Space Museum, Washington, D.C. (ALFRED O. SPORRER COLLECTION)

they were all about. There he met Otto Brodie, a pilot, and R.W. (Shorty) Schroeder, a mechanic, and became so fascinated by flying machines that he spent much of his free time hanging around the field helping pilots and their ground crews in any way he could. He was too practical a man to think that the primitive airplanes of that day had any utilitarian value, although he later recalled that even then he was intrigued by the possibility of hauling mail by air.

A succession of jobs before World War I made Lipsner something of an expert on fleet maintenance and management. He was first hired to manage the fleet of vehicles operated by Albert Pick & Company, a hotel supply firm, and discovered the importance of proper lubrication in keeping the fleet on the road. He later managed the vehicle fleets of two other large corporations, and in 1917 was called to Washington by one of his former employers to solve for the Army the problem of lubricating airplanes. Airplane engines of that time were lubricated primarily with castor oil, an expensive and relatively scarce commodity. The Army estimated that to maintain the anticipated numbers of aircraft it would have in Europe, it would need five million gallons of castor oil—the United States' production for three years. Lipsner's task was to find a substitute.

Lipsner and his staff quickly accomplished that task, but to his regret he discovered that the Army had nothing else for him to do. In his idle time, he began toying with the idea of delivering mail by airplane. He thought advancements made in aircraft since 1910 had made air mail a practical possibility. Furthermore, Congress in 1916 had appropriated $100,000 for air mail experiments, but the money had never been used and the appropriation was to expire June 30, 1918. Early that year Lipsner went to Otto Praeger, second assistant postmaster general, and persuaded him that, with proper maintenance and management, an air mail service could succeed, especially inasmuch as large numbers of pilots and aircraft would become available when the war ended. Praeger was so impressed with the presentation that he had Lipsner detailed from the Army to the Post Office Department and put in charge of establishing the initial air mail route between New York and Washington. Lipsner had that route in operation within a couple of months by using spare Army pilots and planes.

The hangar at Ashburn Field was used to perform maintenance on U.S. Airmail Service planes that flew from Grant Park. (CHICAGO HISTORICAL SOCIETY)

He then turned his attention to the possibility of establishing a longer route. The Post Office liked the idea of the Chicago to New York run and put him in charge. Several pilots in previous years had proved that such a flight could be accomplished, and the Post Office had conducted random air mail experiments for the better part of a decade. The earliest in Chicago occurred in 1912, when Max Lillie flew the mail for a few days between Cicero Field, Elmhurst, and Wheaton. William Robinson later made a flight between Des Moines and Chicago carrying mail, but it wasn't until November 3, 1916, that the feasibility of a New York to Chicago air mail flight was proved by Victor Carlstrom. He took off from Ashburn Field November 2, but was forced down by darkness in Hammondsport, New York, and didn't complete the trip to Governor's Island until the next day. Flying time was eight hours and twenty-six minutes for the 850-mile trip. He carried letters from Charles Dickinson and James Stephens to Alan Hawley, president of the Aero Club of America.

Three weeks later aviatrix Ruth Bancroft Law proved that Carlstrom's flight was no fluke when she set a single-day endurance record of 666 miles over a similar route. She took off from Grant Park at 6:30 a.m. November 19 and landed in Binghamton, New York, six hours and thirty-two minutes later.

Although she carried no mail on that trip, another aviatrix, Katherine Stinson, repeated the journey two years later with a load of mail. Miss Stinson had attempted a non-stop mail flight to New York May 23, 1918, but was forced down when she ran out of fuel 150 miles short of her goal. She was nonetheless awarded the non-stop flight record of 601.7 miles by the Aero Club of America, although her ground route measured 783 miles. She completed the trip to New York City the next day in her Curtiss JN-4 Jenny.[2]

A few months later she applied to Lipsner for a job flying the mail on the Washington-New York route and was turned down. However, she successfully appealed his ruling to the postmaster general and, on September 26, made her first flight for the Air Mail Service, returning the next day. She resigned from the service a few days later and went to Europe to drive an ambulance for the few months that remained of the war.[3]

Despite the fact that the pathfinding flights of Miller and Gardner

130

Castor oil was the principal lubricant used in aircraft engines prior to World War I. Here aviatrix Ruth Law adds some to the engine of her plane in November, 1916, just before taking off from Grant Park to set a long distance flight record between Chicago and New York. (NATIONAL AIR AND SPACE MUSEUM)

The DeHavilland DH-4, principal plane of the U.S. Airmail Service.
(JOHN CASEY COLLECTION)

proved Chicago-New York airmail service feasible, the new agency had neither the planes nor pilots to begin scheduled service. What emerged the next year was a compromise service designed to get mail into the air on that route without the risk involved in flying it at night or over the Allegheny Mountains. The mail was flown between Chicago and Cleveland, where it was transferred to the train for the overnight segment of the trip.

That service began May 15, 1919, when Gardner flew west from Cleveland and Trent C. Fry headed east from Chicago.[4] The new route suffered its first fatality ten days later, when pilot Frank McCusker's DeHavilland DH-4, a plane known among the airmail pilots as the "flaming coffin," caught fire just after takeoff and he fell to his death when he attempted to bail out.[5]

By then, the new service was mired in a number of problems. Lipsner resigned December 6, 1918, after a dispute with Praeger over political interference in the service and plans to buy what Lipsner considered unneeded planes. After the resignation, the Post Office Department was embarrassed by several unsuccessful attempts to get the Chicago-New York route started in the winter of 1918-19. On May 25, 1919, the airmail pilots refused to work—the first such strike in U.S. aviation history—after one of them, E. Hamilton Lee, of Chicago, was fired for refusing to take off with poor visibility.[6] Then the *Chicago Tribune* on June 3 published an article debunking a Post Office contention that the new service to New York saved sixteen hours over the railway postal service. The *Tribune* charged that although the airplanes reached Cleveland in five hours, the mail had to wait there for the train to catch up to carry it on to New York—a net saving of zero. The time saved on westbound mail was only three hours, the newspaper said.

Despite the problems, the Air Mail Service continued, and as the organization became more experienced, improved. On May 15, 1920, service was started between Chicago and Omaha, and on August 16 between Chicago and St. Louis. The agency's long-awaited transcontinental service between New York and San Francisco, via Chicago, started September 8 of that year. On November 7, E. Hamilton Lee flew a test run between Chicago and Minneapolis to check that route, and regular service began December 1.

133

James (Jack) Knight (UNITED AIRLINES)

Thus by the end of 1920 Chicago had become the hub for the nation's fledgling Air Mail Service with routes to New York, Omaha, Minneapolis, and St. Louis. It was a short-lived role, but one that presaged the city's later position as hub for the nation's commercial airline system. The problem in 1920 was that the airplane, which was vulnerable to weather that did not affect train service, did not provide a significant saving of time over the railway postal service, especially on relatively short routes. An economy-minded post-war Congress reduced appropriations for the service, and the Post Office in 1921 dropped all but its transcontinental route.

That route was also plagued with trouble, however. The mail was flown by day and transferred to trains at night, a system that had proved inefficient on the Chicago-New York route two years earlier. Post Office officials realized that if the transcontinental route was to avoid the fate of the others, mail would have to be flown at night to realize the time savings that had been promised. On February 22, 1921, the Air Mail Service attempted coast-to-coast relay flights to prove to Congress that it could be done.

Two planes left New York and two others departed San Francisco, but they almost immediately ran into trouble. One westbound aircraft was forced down just after leaving New York, and the other plane made it as far as Chicago before being grounded by snow. The first plane from the West Coast crashed in Nevada, killing its pilot. Thus within a few hours after the experiment began, only one of the four planes was still in the air, and it completed the trip only because of the heroics of one of its pilots in what has become one of the epic flights in the history of aviation.

The surviving airplane was flown over the legs to Reno, Nevada; Cheyenne, Wyoming; and North Platte, Nebraska, where it was turned over to its next relay pilot, James H. (Jack) Knight, who at 7:50 p.m. headed east. He was to fly the plane the next 276 miles to Omaha, where he was supposed to turn it over to another pilot, but upon landing there at 1:15 a.m., he learned that the pilot and plane that were supposed to meet him had been grounded by snow in Chicago.

Knight decided to continue to Chicago, 435 miles farther east, despite the bitter cold and snow storm which was in progress.

However, he discovered upon his arrival at the refueling station in Des Moines that there was too much snow on the ground to attempt a landing. He continued to the alternate field at Iowa City, only to discover that it was closed; the ground crew, assuming that because the flight from Chicago had been cancelled, the one from Omaha had been too, had gone home. However, the night watchman guided Knight to a safe landing just as he ran out of fuel. They refueled the plane, and Knight gulped some coffee before continuing to Chicago despite the bad weather. Exhausted, he landed at Maywood Field at 8:40 a.m. despite a snow storm in progress and turned the plane over to pilot J.O. Webster. It finally reached New York at 4:50 p.m. that day—thirty-three hours and twenty-one minutes after leaving San Francisco.[7]

Because of Knight's heroics, the flight had demonstrated once and for all the feasibility of day-night service over the transcontinental route, although it was not until January 1, 1924, after signal beacons and airfield lights had been installed, that regular day-night service was begun.

Much of the credit for establishing twenty-four-hour service belonged to another Chicagoan, Colonel Paul Henderson. He was appointed to head the Air Mail Service in January, 1922. Lipsner complained that Henderson's appointment was political because he was the son-in-law of U.S. Representative Martin B. Madden, of Chicago, but Henderson made much of the criticism moot by performing creditably in the job.

With the advancement in aircraft that made scheduled airmail feasible, the major remaining problem for the Post Office was to develop a system of permanent airports that would be available for its planes, as well as for student fliers, daredevils, barnstormers, and commercial operators. In Chicago, the Post Office went through a succession of airports before finding a permanent base. Ashburn was rejected as being too remote, and Grant Park presented too many obstacles to flying despite its central location. By 1920, the Air Mail Service settled on small Checkerboard Field in west suburban Maywood. After a serious fire at Checkerboard, airmail operations were moved to adjacent Maywood Field. However, that airport was not adequate for large scale air operations, and it soon became

Crews load mail aboard a DH-4 at Checkerboard Field in Maywood after the government moved its air mail operations there in the early 1920s. John A. Casey, who later became manager of Chicago's Municipal Airport, is second from right. (JOHN CASEY COLLECTION)

obvious to the Post Office, aviation community, and City of Chicago that a large all-weather airport would have to be built on a site large enough to permit aviation to continue to expand.

1. Both Miller and Gardner were killed in 1920. Miller died after his plane caught fire over New York City, and Gardner while trying to make an emergency landing near Lincoln, Neb.

2. Miss Stinson's dream of making a non-stop flight between Chicago and New York City was realized April 19, 1919, when Army Captain Earl E. White made the trip between Ashburn Field and Hazelhurst, Long Island, in a modified DeHavilland DH-4 in six hours and fifty minutes.

3. Miss Stinson was the first of the four famous flying Stinsons to take to the air, and for six years she showed the world that women were as capable as men in the cockpit. After being taken for a balloon ride in Kansas City in 1911 and for a short flight by one of Tom Benoist's pilots, Tony Jannus, in St. Louis in 1912, Katherine Stinson, then 21, left her home in Canton, Miss., and headed for Cicero Field. There in May, 1912, she persuaded Max Lillie to give her flying lessons and on May 24 applied to the Aero Club of Illinois for a license. She completed the examination July 19 and was given her pilot's certificate. Soon thereafter, her sister, Marjorie, and brothers, Edward, founder of the Stinson Aviation Company which built early commercial airplanes, and Jack, followed her into aviation.

A petite women weighing only one hundred pounds who looked much younger than her 21 years, Miss Stinson was billed in exhibitions as the "Flying Schoolgirl" as she barnstormed the country and quickly became one of the two best known woman pilots of her time. (The other was Ruth Bancroft Law.) She bought for $2,000 a Wright B biplane that had been modified by Lillie and later a biplane by Partridge and Keller that had been fitted with the engine salvaged from Lincoln Beachey's fatal crash.

With Marjorie and Eddie, she opened a flying school in San Antonio, Tex., but her heart was in barnstorming. She left Texas for a tour of Canada in 1916 and later that year went to the Orient. In Japan, she astounded audiences in Yokohama, Tokyo, Nagasaki, Osaka, and Nagoya with her flying in two Chicago-built planes—the Partridge-Keller "Looper" and Laird "Bone Shaker." From Japan, she went to China, where she flew in Peking and Shanghai. Miss Stinson returned to Japan in April, 1917, to learn that the United States had entered World War I, and she immediately left for home.

Once back in the States, she was off on a flying fund-raising drive for the Red Cross in a government Jenny. In early 1918, she attempted a non-stop flight between Chicago and New York City but was forced down with engine trouble in Indiana. Undeterred, she tried again May 23 with a sack of mail as cargo. After a brief fling in the Air Mail Service and a stint as an ambulance driver late in the war, Miss Stinson became ill and moved to New Mexico to recuperate. There is no record that she ever flew again.

She married and settled down in Santa Fe, where she died in 1977.

4. Air service over the entire route began July 1, 1919.

5. The first Air Mail Service fatality occurred Dec. 16, 1918, when Carl B. Smith's DeHavilland crashed at Elizabeth, N.J.

6. Lee was rehired a few days later. Thereafter, the Post Office let local airport managers decide whether the weather would permit flying operations. Lee went on to become a senior pilot for United Airlines, logging 4,400,000 miles without an accident before he retired in 1949.

7. Knight became a pilot for United Airlines and flew 2,400,000 miles before his death Feb. 24, 1945.

The Search for a Municipal Airport

When World War I ended in late 1918, there were only two non-military airports of any significance in Illinois—Ashburn Field and Grant Park. The two major military installations, at Rantoul and Belleville, were too remote for commercial development, and because of the restrictions on wartime civil aviation, the other private facilities in the state were little more than unimproved flying fields. Because of the Aero Club of Illinois, Ashburn was clearly the largest and best airport in the state, although it was not in an ideal location to cope adequately with the frenetic post-war explosion of aviation activity.

Charles Dickinson and other Aero Club members realized that an air mail base at Ashburn would be an important asset to the airport and in early 1919, before the start of regular Chicago-Cleveland-New York air mail service, lobbied hard to have Ashburn chosen as the western terminus for the route.

The Post Office Department ultimately picked Grant Park as its temporary western terminus, but over the next eight years was forced to shift its operations between three airports. Shortly after the Air Mail Service began its flights from Grant Park, an airport opened just west of Chicago in suburban Maywood. The new field was established by Alfred Decker & Cohn, makers of Society Brand Clothes, to permit aerial distribution of its clothing to stores within five hundred miles of Chicago, although initial service was to Kankakee, Champaign, Danville, Valparaiso, and South Bend—a much smaller area. The company also bought two war-surplus JN-4 Jenny biplanes, each capable of speeds of 75 miles an hour, and hired former Army Lieutenant David L. Behncke, who had been in charge of testing and inspecting planes at Chanute Field during the war, to manage the service.[1]

The field was a forty-acre tract at 12th Street (later Roosevelt Road) and the Des Plaines River, and on it the company built a hangar for its two planes. The plane wings were painted with a distinctive checkerboard logotype for high visibility and, because of that, the new airport quickly became known as Checkerboard Field.[2]

The service, typical of commercial aviation ventures of that time, was only marginally successful and did not last long. One of Behncke's initial flights nearly ended in disaster when, on June 6, 1919, he ran into a heavy thunderstorm making a delivery to Valparaiso, Indiana. Attempting to continue his flight to South Bend, Behncke nearly crashed on takeoff and had to fly part of the way only a few hundred feet above the ground to keep his bearings. Nevertheless, he reached South Bend safely, and in a break in the storms, dashed back to Maywood in just forty-five minutes.

Despite the new competition, Dickinson and the Aero Club continued their campaign to obtain city assistance in improving Ashburn. On July 18, club members met with the Chicago Aviation Commission in the Congress Hotel to discuss the city's future aviation needs. Bion J. Arnold, a respected consulting engineer and Aero Club member, urged on behalf of the club that an all-weather airport be established. "We should have a large landing field, plainly marked and equipped with sounding apparatus so that even on cloudy days when vision is impaired, aviators would know where to land. The ideal field should be seen, felt, and heard. Grant Park, though not bad on a perfect day, is unsuited at present for that purpose. It cannot be readily found. We must have a capacious field that can be used winter or summer," Arnold said.[3] E. H. Bennett, City Plan Commission engineer, agreed that Grant Park was not a desirable airport, as did

This early aerial photo shows both Maywood (center) and Checkerboard fields on either side of First Avenue. Maywood's two runways
can be clearly seen. Checkerboard (upper right) is seen just above the
racktrack oval. (CHICAGO TRIBUNE)

Walter J. Smith posed for this photograph at Checkerboard Field on Sept. 6, 1922, two days before he was killed at Indianapolis when his DH-4 went into a spin after takeoff. (UNITED AIRLINES)

the eleven aldermen attending the meeting. Bennett even went so far as to say that Ashburn would be a suitable replacement, with improvements.

It appeared that, as a result of the July 18 meeting, the Aero Club had convinced the city to invest in Ashburn as the city's airport of the future. However, the Ashburn campaign lost steam three days later when the *Wingfoot* disaster caused some aldermen who had enthusiastically supported aviation expansion July 18 to denounce it as unsafe. The Aero Club's campaign for an improved Ashburn quickly turned into a defensive strategy to prevent the City Council from legislating aviation out of existence in Chicago.

The final blow to Ashburn's future occurred the next January (1920), when the Post Office Department shifted its Air Mail Service base from Grant Park to Checkerboard Field. When Alfred Decker & Cohn discontinued its aerial delivery service in early 1920, Behncke bought the company's two airplanes and continued to operate Checkerboard as a commercial airport. The beginning of the Air Mail Service flights there that year gave Behncke a sufficient revenue base to make the transition.[4]

Checkerboard continued to grow in importance, despite its relatively small size, as the Air Mail Service expanded. Regular service to Omaha began May 15, 1920, and four days later Behncke signed a lease for $500 a year for an additional twenty acres to expand the airport. He also operated Checkerboard Airplane Service, offering airplane rides, exhibition flying, aerial photography, and air express service, and hired Bert R. Blair as assistant manager and Louis E. Meyer as a mechanic. The Post Office added routes to St. Louis August 16 and Minneapolis December 1.

Despite the loss of the air mail, Ashburn continued to flourish under Aero Club sponsorship. Elmer Partridge and Henry Keller continued to build their airplanes there, and Ralph C. Diggins opened an aviation school there in 1920 to train pilots. He sold it in 1923 to James Levy Aircraft Company, which kept the school at Ashburn, and later that year Matty Laird returned to Chicago from Wichita, Kansas, to start the E.M. Laird Airplane Company. Ashburn remained as the home base for most of the private pilots in the Chicago area, as well as the Aero Club's center of activities.

Meanwhile, Checkerboard had run into difficulty. Congress refused to appropriate sufficient funds for the Air Mail Service to operate anything but its transcontinental route, and on June 30, 1921, the routes to Minneapolis and St. Louis were discontinued. Some time thereafter, most of the airport's buildings were razed in a fire. The Post Office promptly moved its air mail operations across First Avenue to government-owned land. That became Maywood Airport, the air mail terminal in Chicago until 1927. Behncke continued to operate Checkerboard until 1923, when he sold out to Wilfred Alonzo (Tony) Yackey, a former air mail pilot who had founded Yackey Aircraft Company to specialize in the rebuilding of surplus military aircraft for commercial use, especially the French-built Brequet bombers. They were rebuilt and sold as Yackey Transports, and the company also built a two-seat biplane called the Yackey Sport. Checkerboard was abandoned in 1928 after Yackey died in a plane crash.[5]

Despite its use by the Air Mail Service, Maywood Field was too small to survive long. It was adequate for the government's limited transcontinental air mail service but not for the rapid expansion of commercial activity that occurred in 1926 when the Post Office Department began awarding air mail contracts to private operators. When pilot Charles A. Lindbergh on April 15, 1926, made Chicago's first non-government air mail flight from Maywood in a Robertson Aircraft Corporation plane, it was already a foregone conclusion that Maywood was doomed.

Long before that flight it had become obvious to the Chicago political establishment that, if the city intended to remain a major aviation center, a modern airport would have to be built on a site large enough to permit considerable growth. However, the first approach Chicago adopted was to attempt to build several smaller airports around the city. This was largely the result of a lobbying effort by Dickinson to improve facilities available to private pilots. On Aero Club stationery, Dickinson wrote to Dan Ryan, president of the Cook County Forest Preserve District, urging that the county use some of its recently acquired recreation sites for airports. Dickinson mentioned in his letter that there were already two airports on county land—apparently including Cook County Airport, at Irving Park Road just east of River Road, and Cook County Airport Number

146

This stand was used for testing Liberty engines at Maywood Field in
the mid 1920s. (JOHN CASEY COLLECTION)

Chicago Aero Park, of which this photograph was taken about 1926, later became Chicago Municipal and, still later, Chicago Midway Airport. The hangar at the lower corner of the field was built by Phillip Kemp, who operated four planes there. (CITY OF CHICAGO)

Two, just south of Checkerboard Field in Maywood.

The city's 1922 airport plan also called for building a number of flying fields at several sites on the fringes of the city. Mayor William Hale Thompson, after attending the Detroit convention of the National Aeronautic Association in 1922, also contemplated a $10-million island airport in Lake Michigan just off the Field Museum and linked to the mainland by a tunnel.[6]

The only one of those airports built as envisioned was a flying field on a square mile of open land at 63rd Street and Cicero Avenue. It was dedicated by the City Aeronautical Bureau October 1, 1922, and although it was fated in little more than a decade to become the busiest airport on earth, it was used initially for practice landings by pilots from Ashburn and Maywood. The next year it acquired at least one tenant, Chicago Air Park Company, a firm offering flying lessons and aerial photography services.

In the meantime, the pressure from the U.S. Post Office Department to develop all weather airports increased. That agency by 1922 was already deeply involved in planning the facilities necessary for a night route between Chicago and San Francisco. Under Chicagoan Paul Henderson's direction, the Post Office in 1923 began installing the first of 289 signal beacons at twenty-five-mile intervals between Chicago and Cheyenne, Wyoming, and renting emergency air strips at strategic locations along the route. The fields were equipped with emergency lighting, rotating electric beacons, boundary markers, and telephones. The navigation beacons were, of course, available to anyone flying that route, not just air mail pilots.[7]

With most of the new equipment in place, the Post Office on July 1, 1924, began around-the-clock service between New York and San Francisco, via Chicago, on a thirty-day trial basis. The service was so successful that it was continued at the end of the trial period.

The success of the service, the continued expansion of aviation, the possibility that commercial airlines would be formed within the next few years, and the increasing pressure from the aviation community for an all-weather airport convinced many of Chicago's civic leaders that the city would have to build a municipal airport, not just a group of small fields scattered around the city. Charles H. Wacker, chairman of the Chicago Plan Commission, on July 15—two weeks after the transcontinental service started—asked the City Council to lease from the Board of Education an agricultural tract bounded by Cicero Avenue, 55th Street, Central Avenue, and 63rd Street on the South to be developed "as a Municipal Airplane Landing Field."[8] The Plan Commission had endorsed the idea June 24 because the tract " is practically the only remaining site of its size, kind, and availability within the City of Chicago."

Four months later, the City Council unanimously adopted a resolution offered by Alderman Dorsey Crowe to have the council's Committee on Public Works and Recreation find a location for a new public airport in Chicago.[9] Ashburn, which remained as the area's most important airport, was probably never seriously considered as the site of the proposed new municipal field. That must have been obvious to Dickinson, for in 1925 he sold all but 80 acres of the original 640 acres at Ashburn to be subdivided.[10]

The relatively primitive conditions there made Laird's airplane manufacturing operation especially difficult, and in 1925 he took the step that apparently forced the city's hand in acquiring a municipal airport. Laird wrote to the Board of Education asking to lease the existing field at 63rd Street and Cicero Avenue so he could locate his aircraft factory there. The board turned down his request, forcing him to build at 4500 W. 83rd Street, on the north edge of Ashburn Field, but within a month Crowe introduced in the City Council an ordinance authorizing the city to negotiate with the Board of Education for the 63rd Street and Cicero Avenue site.[11]

Crowe was undoubtedly as much influenced by the February 2, 1925 signing by President Calvin Coolidge of the Kelly Act turning over the transportation of air mail from the Post Office to private contractors as he was by Laird's interest in the site. The Kelly Act authorized the postmaster general to grant air mail contracts to private companies on a low bid basis. The act, in effect, resulted in the establishment of the modern airlines, and at the time was interpreted to mean that Chicago would get additional air mail routes linking it to cities not then on the Post Office Department's transcontinental route.

The City Council, acting with unusual speed, unanimously approved Crowe's ordinance April 1. It authorized the city to sign a twenty-five year lease with the Board of Education for as much as $6 an acre for the new airport. Two days later, Philip G. Kemp, chairman of Mayor William E.Dever's Aero Commission, reached an agreement with the Board of Education on a twenty-five-year lease on 300 acres. Early the next year, the City Council approved $25,000 for improvements to the field and $1,560 in annual rent payments.[12]

Undoubtedly contributing to the haste with which the city acted was the speed of the Post Office in implementing the Kelly Act. By October 2, 1925, about eight months after the act was signed into law, the Post Office awarded the first five air mail contracts,[13] including those for routes serving Chicago, Dallas, St. Louis, Detroit, and Cleveland. The first Chicago company to bid successfully on the new routes was National Air Transport, which had been formed the previous May 21 with the financial backing of such prominent Chicagoans as John Mitchell Jr., Marshall Field, William Wrigley, Jr., and Philip D. and Lester Armour. The airline promptly hired Henderson away from the Air Mail Service to be its general manager.[14]

Although its route was submitted for bids two weeks after the others, Ford Motor Company, which had been awarded the Chicago-Detroit-Cleveland segment, was the first of the new airlines to get into operation. Its first plane left Maywood Field at 1:45 p.m. February 15, 1926, for Detroit. The first N.A.T. aircraft to Chicago arrived at Maywood February 21 en route to Kansas City from the Curtiss factory in Buffalo, New York. It carried no cargo, however.

On May 8, 1926, Chicago's new Municipal Airport, at 59th Street and Cicero Avenue, officially opened with a great deal of hoopla but very little business. The first airplane to land there was a Curtiss Carrier Pigeon owned by N.A.T. and flown by Edmund Marucha from Maywood Field for the ceremony.[15] The plane, christened *Miss Chicago* during the ceremony, finally took off from Maywood May 12 with N.A.T.'s first load of mail for Dallas.

In the round of speeches that followed the plane's arrival at the Municipal Airport dedication, Crowe predicted that the airport would have an important effect on commerce, and William R. Hayes, president of the Chicago Association of Commerce, praised the financiers who made N.A.T. possible with $500,000 in capital. Miss Marguerite Foster, 15, daughter of George Foster, chairman of the

151

Edmund Muchara flew this National Air Transport Carrier Pigeon to
the dedication of Chicago's new Municipal Airport on May 8, 1926.
(CHICAGO TRIBUNE)

Association's aviation committee, christened the $30,000 *Miss Chicago* and released four carrier pigeons carrying messages to officials in Washington.

After the ceremony, Marucha and Edgar Van Vechten, an N.A.T. employee, took off in *Miss Chicago* to return to Maywood. Municipal Airport returned to the almost deserted condition that had characterized it since 1922 and would characterize it for another year and a half. Municipal Airport did not have an appreciable amount of traffic until after December 1, 1927, when all air mail flights were transferred there from Maywood.[16]

In a few years, however, Chicago's civic boosters would be able to call Municipal Airport the "world's busiest," and in 1959, its busiest year, more than ten million airline passengers passed through it. By then it had been renamed Midway Airport for the World War II naval battle.

1. Behncke later flew for Northwest and United airlines and founded the Air Line Pilots Association.

2. The airport was officially opened at 11 a.m. June 3, 1919.

3. *Chicago Tribune*, July 19, 1919.

4. The first Air Mail Service test flight at Checkerboard Field was Jan. 8, 1920, to Omaha.

5. Yackey died Oct. 4, 1927, and the land was later sold to the Cook County Forest Preserve District.

6. *Greater Chicago Magazine*, November, 1922. It should be noted that Thompson's proposed airport in the lake was later developed as Meigs Field, a small airport for general aviation and commuter airlines linked to the mainland by a half-mile causeway. In the late 1960s and early 1970s, Mayor Richard J. Daley enthusiastically endorsed a plan to build a major jetport on a man-made island in Lake Michigan, but the idea was dropped because of the high cost and environmental objections.

7. Dickinson demonstrated the feasibility of night flying between Chicago and New York July 27, 1923, when he made the non-stop trip in a single-engine plane flown by Eddie Stinson.

8. Charles H. Wacker letter of July 15, 1924, in City Council Journal.

9. City Council Journal, Oct. 22, 1924.

10. Even after the opening of Municipal Airport in 1926, Ashburn remained the area's busiest airport, and probably its best equipped. It was the site of the area's two best flying schools, one of which was operated by Partridge and Keller; Laird's airplane factory; a National Guard unit equipped with two

planes; and approximately forty privately owned aircraft. Ashburn had at least four wooden hangars, a welding shop, a shop for recovering wings, a twenty-five-bed bunkhouse for students, and a dining hall. Room and board for students in those days was $12 a week. However, the airport suffered from the lack of utilities. Electrical power was provided by a generator, a well and windmill provided water, and the only plumbing consisted of outhouses.

11. City Council Journal of March 25, 1925.

12. City Council Journal of Jan. 16, 1926.

13. The Robertson Aircraft Corporation, of St. Louis, was awarded the Chicago-St. Louis route by the Post Office; National Air Transport received the Chicago-Dallas route; Western Air Express the Salt Lake City-Los Angeles route; Varney Air Lines the route between Pasco, Wash., Boise, Idaho, and Elko, Nev.; and Colonial Air Lines the Boston-Hartford-New York route. Two weeks later, the Chicago-Detroit-Cleveland route was awarded to Ford Motor Co.

14. National Air Transport was one of the principals of several carriers later merged into United Airlines.

15. The second plane to land at Municipal Airport was probably a government aircraft flown by Lieutenant Merrill Mann and carrying Alderman Crowe. It flew to Municipal from Ashburn Field, only about three miles away.

16. Dec. 1, 1927, is often erroneously given as the date Municipal Airport officially opened. The continuous use of the site as an airport can be traced to Oct. 1, 1922, although it was not officially dedicated under the name Municipal Airport until May 8, 1926. There appears from various records to have been aviation activity on the site before 1922, although it was not continuously used as a flying field.

Epilogue

"My only wish is to see Chicago become the
center of American flying."
—Charles Dickinson, 1923.

In some respects, Dickinson's wish became a reality within the decade in which it was spoken. By the end of 1926, the trends that were to dominate American aviation for the next thirty years were already in evidence. The aircraft manufacturing industry was gravitating toward the West Coast, and the federal government had taken its first step, albeit small, toward the regulation of aviation. The nuclei of what would become the commercial airlines were in existence, and Chicago was already fitting into its role as the principal crossroads of aviation—the airlines' hub of operations.

Within two years of 1926, Municipal Airport first became the busiest flying field in the nation, then the busiest in the world. As the airplanes grew larger, safer, and more comfortable to passengers, Midway Airport, as it had by then been renamed, became so inundated with humanity and aircraft that Chicago had to build yet another, larger airport. In the meantime, the federal government was forced to devise a control system just to direct traffic in the air around Midway.

Bessie Coleman, first black woman to obtain a pilot's license, went from Chicago to France to learn to fly. She returned in 1921 and put on an air show over Checkerboard Field. She was killed on April 30, 1926, while practicing for an air show in Florida. (BESSIE COLEMAN FAMILY)

The private mail carriers, which began flying in 1926, grew from small companies headquartered in unused corners of airplane hangars and operating a few single-engine biplanes flown by barnstormers or World War I veterans into giant corporations operating fleets of hundreds of planes to all corners of the nation. National Air Transport, which began operations with a few Curtiss Carrier Pigeons in 1926, ultimately grew into United Airlines, which in later years launched into production such planes as the 727 and 767 with multi-million-dollar orders.

Thus 1926 marked the end of aviation's first era in Chicago. The magnificent men who took to the skies in their flying machines dwindled in importance as aviation became dominated first by the professional managers, then by committees of lawyers, accountants, technicians, and bureaucrats. It was still possible for one person to dominate some aspect of aviation, but only by mastering the intricacies of corporate management, government regulation, and high finance.

With the opening of Municipal Airport and the formation of the commercial airlines, the role of the Aero Club of Illinois diminished further. Altough it continued in existence until after Dickinson's death in 1935, it never again was the dominant force it had once been in Chicago aviation. No longer needed, it simply disappeared. No one knows for sure when.

But Dickinson and the Aero Club both lived long enough to see the fulfillment of their dream that Chicago would be a center of American aviation.

Bibliography

The following are publications of interest to students of Chicago aviation. General works on aviation which allude to events in Chicago are too numerous to mention.

1. Octave Chanute, *Progress in Flying Machines*, Lorenz & Herweg, Long Beach, Cal. 1977. (Reprint.)

2. Howard L. Scamehorn, *Balloons to Jets*, Henry Regnery Co., Chicago, 1951.

3. Benjamin B. Lipsner, *The Air Mail: Jennys to Jets*, Wilcox and Follett, Chicago, 1956.

4. Zenon Hansen, *The Goodyear Airships*, Airship International Press, Bloomington, Ill., 1977.

5. James L. Shock, *American Airship Bases and Facilities*, a manuscript planned for publication by Airship International Press, Bloomington, Ill.

6. Nick A. Komons, *Bonfires to Beacons: Federal Aviation Policy Under The Air Commerce Act 1916-38*, U.S. Department of Transportation, 1978.

7. John W. Underwood, *The Stinsons*, Heritage Press, Glendale, Cal., 1976.

Index

Aero Club of America, 25, 28, 50, 59, 60, 61, 65, 67, 68f, 119, 120, 130.
Aero Club of Illinois, 8f, 19, 52, 59, 60, 61, 63, 64, 67, 69f, 71, 75, 83, 85, 90, 102, 103, 110, 119, 138f, 141, 142, 145.
    Organized, 23, 89.
    Flying field, 26, 45, 52, 54, 56, 63, 81.
    Dealings with Wright brothers, 27.
    Air shows, 27, 28, 29.
    Files, 30f, 56f, 68f, 85, 111f.
    Dispute with Lougheed, 40.
    Officers, 56f, 110.
    War activities, 102, 105.
Aero Club of Paris, 16.
Aeronautique Club of Chicago, 6, 8f.
Air Commerce Act (U.S.) of 1926, 120.
Air Line Pilots Association, 94, 155f.
Air Mail Act (U.S.) of 1925, 122.
Akron, O., 113, 114.
Albany, N.Y., 24.
Alfred, Decker & Cohn Co., 142, 145.
Algonac, Mich., 2.
Allegheny Mountains, 125, 126, 133.
Allen, A. Livingstone, 105.
America Defender airplane, 90, 98f, 103.
American Airways, 110.
American Society of Civil Engineers, 18.

Anderson, Charles P, 111f.
Armour & Company, 102.
Armour, Lester, 151
Armour, Philip D., 151.
Armstrong, William J., 111f.
Arnold, Bion J., 75, 83, 142.
Ashburn Field, 71, 83, 85, 87, 91, 93, 94, 98, 98f, 105, 106, 120, 130, 136, 138f, 141, 142, 145, 149, 150, 156f.
Atchison, Topeka & Santa Fe Railway, 19.
Atwood, Harry, 36, 43f, 72.
Atwood, Ont., 6.
Auditorium Theater, 34.
Ava, O., 122.
Avery, William A., 13.

B-1 (blimp), 113.
Badger, William, 37, 43f.
Baldwin, Fredrick W., 21f.
Ballough, Ervin E. (Eddie), 94, 97, 98.
Baker, John M., 111f.
Barnum, P.T., 1.
Barrett, Charles E., 24.
Barrier, Rene, 29.
Bartholf, Herbert B., 111f.
Bates, Carl S., 23, 47.
Beachey, Lincoln, 34, 37, 38, 41f, 42f, 60, 61, 63, 72, 81, 138f.
Beatty, G.W., 38, 40, 42f.
Behncke, David L., 94, 142, 145, 146.
Beifeld, Joseph, 47
Bell, Alexander Graham, 21f.
Belleville, Ill., 111f, 141.

159

161

162

Wichita, Kan., 145.
Wild, Horace B., 6, 8f, 47.
Wilder, Emery, 111.
Willard, Charles, 29, 50.
Wilson, Woodrow, 120, 125.
Wingfoot Air Express (blimp), 85,
91, 114, 117, 118, 119, 120, 145.
Wingfoot Lake, O., 113, 114.
Winslow, Alan F., 112f.
Wise, John, 6.
Witmer, Charles G., 43f, 79.
Wolff, Alfred, 111, 112f.
Wood, G. F. Campbell, 67, 68f.
World's Columbian Exposition, 12.
World War I, 3, 60, 65, 68f, 71, 72,
91, 101, 105, 109, 111f, 120, 128,
138f, 141.
World War II, 106, 110, 153.
Worrel, Rodney K., 30f.

Wright B biplane, 138f.
Wright brothers, 8, 9, 11, 15, 19f,
20f, 27, 28, 29, 40, 43, 48, 56f, 60,
101.
Wright, Katharine, 16.
Wright, Orville, 15, 27, 60, 65.
Wright, Wilbur, 15, 19f, 48, 68f.
  Wright patent, 27.
  Wright Company, 28, 30f, 38,
40.
Wrigley, Philip K., 111.
Wrigley, William Jr., 151.

Yackey *Sport* (airplane), 146.
Yackey, Tony, 94, 146, 155f.
Yackey transports, 146.
Ye Ham, 98f.
Yokohama, Japan, 138f.
Young, William C., 118.